BALANCE

BALANCE

A Book for Those Who Want to Love God,
Others, and Themselves.

By: Michael Starling

XULON PRESS

Xulon Press
2301 Lucien Way #415
Maitland, FL 32751
407.339.4217
www.xulonpress.com

Paperback ISBN-13: 978-1-66284-124-8
Ebook ISBN-13: 978-1-66284-125-5

TABLE OF CONTENTS

—

INTRODUCTION

———

"A false balance is an abomination to the LORD, but a just weight is His delight." Proverbs 11:1

In my last book, *No Filter: A Beginner's Guidebook for Anyone Who has Ever Hated God, Others, or Themselves*, I mainly dealt with those who were gladly outside the church or resented being inside the church. However, even though I received positive feedback by those who read it, those who read it were those who were gladly inside the church, and they were my friends, family, or fellow church members. Although they appreciated how I was able to help them to enter the mind of those who are angry, skeptical, and even suicidal, I realized something: Such a title is a title that will in all likelihood repulse anyone within the demographic I was hoping to reach.

For why would such people want to read a book that deals with topics they want to avoid thinking about? If anyone of that demographic was ever going to bother reading such a book, it would be at the recommendation of those who were gladly inside the church. To which, I felt compelled to write this book, a book for those who are gladly within the church and want to continue growing in their faith. Inasmuch, it would help to kill two birds with one stone: dealing with subjects and controversies within the church itself, while also raising awareness of my other book to help those who need it.

Nevertheless, which is more important? Reaching the lost and hurting, or developing a healthy church? Should we focus all our efforts into evangelism and reaching the lost, putting theological and disciplinary issues aside for the sake of "unity", or do we become a monastery on a mountain top in the middle of nowhere until we have every single issue sorted out? In this book, I hope to deal with such extremes and almost everything in between in a fair and balanced manner.

For as the verse in the beginning of this introduction suggests, God wants us to be fair and impartial when weighing the issues. Furthermore, if Jesus felt compelled to flip over a table, fashion a whip, and chase the money changers out of the temple for deceiving and robbing the people, I would hate to see Him react at the way many Christians handle controversy. For there are many prominent Christians in whom I agree with their positions, but I hate the way in which they misrepresent their opposition. Furthermore, so many Christians have a different set of rules for the opposition than they have for themselves, and they often make up the rules as they go.

Inasmuch, not everyone agrees to what is to be considered "fair". Some only consider it fair if everyone gets what they want, while others only think it fair for themselves to get what they want while the opposition receives nothing, not even pity. However, not everyone can get what they want, and there are those who want it all who in fact should receive nothing. Fairness, according to the Bible, is dependent on how God sees the subject or controversy, not ourselves. However, if we fear God, which is the beginning of wisdom, then we will start to see fairness as God sees it. Yet, even so, there will always be those who don't fear God, nor have any wisdom, who will not be satisfied until they've shed the entirety of the opposition's blood. Not only that, but they will consider themselves to be approved by God in doing so.

How are we to deal with such people? Firstly, we have to agree that Scripture is the final authority by which we view the world and its sorrows. Secondly, we have to *know* what the Scripture says. Thirdly, we have to *surrender* to what the Scripture says, regardless as to how it affects our current lives, desires, or positions on theology, politics, or any other subject. Fourthly, we must seek to conform the rest of the church to that understanding. Fifthly, we shouldn't be so quick to discipline or excommunicate everyone who doesn't see things Biblically. Sixthly, we must exercise church discipline and excommunication, when necessary, regardless of how dear to our hearts the one being disciplined is to us.

However, is it possible to focus on such endeavors without forsaking the great commission? Yes. For the church in the days of the Apostles had plenty of theological and holiness issues, but they didn't forsake preaching the Gospel to the lost. However, even Paul recognized the importance of unity under right theology and expectations in personal holiness if the pagan world was going to take us seriously. Inasmuch, I hope to deal with that tension in this book.

Now, I'm not opposed to calling heretics out by name, but I choose not to in this book, although I give descriptions of some of them and their situations to which anyone who pays attention to such things should be able to figure out who I'm referring to. For there are plenty of preachers and teachers in whom I'm convinced are not only in simple error, but are wolves in sheep's clothing, in whom there are those who consider those preachers and teachers to be the golden standard. If I was to call them out by name, then many people will throw the book away before they have even bothered to read my rebuke.

Inasmuch, it's not so much the *person* who's deadly, but their *teaching*. For a teaching can spread much further and for far longer than a single individual. For a torch isn't what sets the forest on fire, but the flame the torch carries. If you extinguish the flame, the torch is harmless. Yes, Jesus said that if anyone causes others to stumble that it would be better for them to have a millstone tied to their neck and thrown into the sea. However, even if the torch is tossed into the sea, it does nothing to stop the spread of what has already been set ablaze.

Thus, even if every single false teacher was to drop dead, it would do nothing about what they have taught if there are thousands if not millions who believe the teaching. To which, some of them will rise to the occasion and replace the fallen false-prophet, and could possibly be even worse than the devils we knew. Nevertheless, there are plenty of Christians in which I'm thoroughly convinced are truly born-again who themselves are thoroughly convinced that such teachers are truly born-again, if not legitimate Apostles and prophets.

However, such teachers and teachings are not my only concern. Some so-called Christians have social and political opinions in which are not only unbiblical, but often held to the same if not higher esteem as the Bible, itself. Not only that, but they often resort to the same tactics as false-teachers within the church, and even teachers that I once highly esteemed have become captivated by such grand narratives and philosophies.

I now shutter whenever I hear a Christian, or anyone for that matter, claim that they want to be "on the right of history!" For such people are almost always on the *wrong* side of history, for they almost always join the wrong side of the debate. They don't care about God and truth as much as they do "relevance". They are quick to defend the enemies of God from the harshness of Christian rhetoric, but hardly ever, if ever at all, do they call out the sin of the world. The false prophets of Scripture always wanted the limelight, whereas the true prophets were typically reluctant at first and only spoke out when they felt they had no other choice, despite receiving public shame, persecution, and death at the hands of the people of whom the false prophet defended.

Furthermore, the false prophet often stands aside whenever the enemies of God attack the children of God, if not help to lead the charge, themselves. They often excuse the actions of the enemies of God because "their heart was in the right place," or "it was only because the Christians provoked them," or "they don't know any better". Inasmuch, the Christian is always in the wrong and the non-Christian is always in the right. The harshness of Christian rhetoric is worse than non-Christian violence. Christian tone is worse than non-Christian torture. And as one theologian put it, as long as Christians are convinced that the Kingdom of God is a nice family picnic and not a war with the demonic forces of evil, they too will be convinced of the false prophet's heresies and join in on the rebuke against Christian soldiers for fighting a battle instead of passing the butter.

Now, I learned many years ago to not pay so much attention to what is being said, but the attitude and behavior of the one who said it. I would read in the gospels of how Jesus knew the Pharisee's questions were a trap. For the longest time I thought such abilities were only possible by His ability to read minds. However, I've since learned that if you pay attention to the inflections in people's voices and the movements, gestures, and posturing they make with their bodies, you can tell when someone isn't sincere. You may not know what their exact motives are in asking the question, but you can tell they don't truly care for the answer. You may not know what they truly believe, but you know they don't believe the statement they've given you.

That's why I resent the sentiment that Christians should have nothing to do with psychology, saying it's a worldly profession and science. Although I briefly deal with such thinking later, I want to say now that even a blind squirrel finds a nut every now and then. Furthermore, understanding body language, vocal patterns, basic motives, and common behaviors, can possibly save your life one day, or at least spare you a lot of heartache.

I learned the hard way to never take someone at their word, no matter how close they were to me. For sociopaths (a fancy way of saying "unrepentant sinners") take great care to build relationships with their victims so as to build their trust. Furthermore, whenever previous victims tried to warn me of their ways, I would dismiss it. Either I thought the sociopaths to be too kind to be capable of such a thing, or I brushed it off as "Nobody's perfect and we all have our moments". However, when those accusations were coming from their own children and relatives, and the stories were getting worse, after a while I began to grow concerned. When I confronted the sociopaths, they often admitted to the accusations, but justified them as "No one's perfect" or "What they did to me was worse". Sound familiar?

Furthermore, some of them claimed their victims to be worse than themselves simply because they had the audacity to call them out on it. "I'm their parent!" or "I'm their sibling!" or "What about all the times I did something nice for them? Doesn't that count for *anything*? Those ungrateful [expletives]!" If they were willing to treat their own children or family that way, why should I believe they wouldn't do the same to me? If they were so quick to throw their own family under the bus for having the audacity to tell them "No", what would they do to *me*?

Oh, but they promise to *never* do that to me! I'm their buddy! We've known each other for years! Yeah, but you've known your family for longer. You keep promising *them* to never do it again, and then do it again once they've let their guard down. And like the book of Judges, again they did what was evil in the sight of the Lord! However, many times, I didn't discover these people for who they were until they did it to me, or at least I didn't take the warnings seriously until it happened to me. Fool me once, shame on you. Fool me twice, shame on me. Fool me 300 times, I don't care for you to be a part of my life anymore. And after a while, I can actually predict what will happen before it happens. For even if their excuses change, their actions don't, nor does the giving of excuses.

Nevertheless, when it comes to current family, friends, and associates, I've developed a love for the application of Occam's razor, which states that the simplest explanation is often the most likely. Even when dealing with someone I'm close to, if something feels off about the situation, I say to myself, "If this person was a complete stranger, what would I assume about them?" If the answer is, for example, "I would assume they were hiding something," then that's the most likely answer.

Now, whether they're hiding nefarious ulterior motives, hiding their own suspicion of myself, hiding the fact that they're uncomfortable with the topic, or hiding the fact that they need to use the restroom, they're still hiding something. Nevertheless, unless you're a highly trained actor who knows how to put on a poker face, then even a loved one will give away the same "tells" as a stranger would. Such is not only true when they're hiding something, but when it comes to all feelings and behaviors.

Typically, compulsive liars manifest themselves with a wide-eyed disbelief in your unbelief of their story, with a high-pitched inflection in their voice, saying, "Why would I lie! I swear to God!" Typically, they're actually surprised you didn't believe the story they worked so hard on and thought was a cleverly-crafted, open-and-shut case. However, even someone who's telling the truth may have the same reaction, to which, both may even resort to tears.

How do you spot the difference? *Typically*, the one who is telling the truth will continue to give more details without a moment's pause, whereas the liar will *typically* be taken aback and begin to stumble over their words as they try to fabricate something new. Or, they will simply repeatedly scream, "I can't believe you don't believe me!" or "What an [insult] you are for not believing me!" rather than giving more details. Nevertheless, if family and friends are willing to take advantage of you, why should you trust a complete stranger, no matter who they are?

Inasmuch, whether it's due to unrepentant sin, or an actual chemical imbalance, I eventually don't care why people behave the way they do if they insist on making my life miserable for their own sakes. Besides, given that the soul and body are connected, I'm sure that certain sins produce certain chemicals in the brain that can become addictive or pattern producing. Looking at porn for the first time produces dopamine, but that doesn't excuse you to lust. Committing a crime for the first time produces an adrenaline rush, but that doesn't excuse you for committing the crime. If you continue to not repent of your porn or your crimes, it becomes an addiction or lifestyle, each time becoming easier than the next. For you crave that next hit of dopamine, or that next adrenaline rush.

However, your senses also become dulled and you will eventually give in to such sins without a moment's pause. You also become defensive and justify your actions. And the more depraved you become, the more defensive you become and the more justified you feel. As Romans 1 says, you become senseless in your reasonings and your heart is darkened, and God gives you over to a depraved mind. And it's the same with those who practice lying, whether it be family, friends, associates, or even "men of God".

For 1 Timothy 4: 1-2 says, "But the Spirit explicitly says that in later times some will fall away from the faith, paying attention to

deceitful spirits and teachings of demons, <u>by means of the hypoc-</u>
<u>risy of liars seared in their own conscience as with a branding</u>
<u>iron</u>." If you devote yourself to lying and refuse to repent, your
conscience will become void of guilt and discernment. You may
even start to believe your own lies, in which, your fate may very
well be sealed. That's why it's detrimental to a person's well-being
to dismiss such behavior as a chemical imbalance, a behavior disorder, or whatever medical or psychiatric term you want to use.
The last thing we need a "sociopath" or "narcissist" or "borderline
personality disorder" to hear is the phrase "You can't blame them
for their actions. They can't help it." Believe me, they will be sure
to excuse every "episode" from there on out with a doctor's note.

Inasmuch, I remember watching a certain pastor for the first
time and I was immediately unnerved by him, although I couldn't
figure out why at the time. I later realized a coworker of mine
would constantly jerk his head slightly to the side whenever he
started to brag about an accomplishment at work, and he looked
similar to the man in question. When I later watched a video Bible
study of his, he jerked his head the same way and for the same
reason, especially when bragging about how he "tricked" his wife
into going on a date with him. I also noticed he often had the
same twitch whenever the crowd applauded him, along with the
same smirk. As I got to know more about his beliefs, he turned
out to have far greater issues than an ego, and his ego is massive.
Where there's smoke, there's fire. However, instead of dismissing
himself with a doctor's note, he dismisses himself as being commanded to act and teach in such a manner by the authority and
direct revelation of God Himself!

Nevertheless, I often notice the same ego in the people who call
this man (and similar types) out on their podcasts, radio broad-
casts, or YouTube channels. Such egos are typically expressed in
their clickbait titles, whacky sound effects, and "slam dunk" rebut-
tals [Queue the "Thug Life" music and sunglasses animation]. They

often seem more focused on being comedians than Christlike. Yes, the word of God is sharper than any two-edged sword, but that's a far cry from being "edgy" in the name of God. Yes, Jesus Himself is known to have used sarcasm and even insults when dealing with His opponents. However, the fact you're only able to point to a handful of verses in which He responded in such a manner shows that it wasn't His natural language or mode of communication. Nevertheless, even if the Wolf-spotter is willing to recognize their attitude, they often justify it because it's not as bad as what the Wolf is doing or teaching (I guess the thief is justified in his stealing because he stole from the murderer). Inasmuch, they feel as if they're excused to act as they do by the written Word of God that is plain for all to see! But I digress.

Although I do not talk about every Christian concern, controversy, or conspiracy in this book, I should be able to at least help get the ball rolling in the right direction and attitude. Besides, even if I'm wrong, it doesn't mean you're right. Even if my own position is somehow completely false, it doesn't mean your own interpretation is 100% accurate. And even your belief is indeed 100% accurate, you can still have the completely wrong attitude. If you can't even finish reading this book before throwing it away and disregarding anything and/or everything I said up until that point, then I doubt you will ever be able to comprehend your opposition, much less win them over with any measure of grace, if you can win them over at all. And even if you do win them over, they are likely to be as obnoxious as yourselves, if not more so.

"Woe to you, scribes and Pharisees, hypocrites, because you travel around on sea and land to make one proselyte; and when he becomes one, you make him *twice* as much a son of hell as yourselves." Matthew 23:15

BELIAL VS BEREANS

In *No Filter*, in the final chapter, I talked a bit about the sons of Eli. There was an aspect of that story that I really wanted to dive into, but I thought it would be too distracting to the overall message of that chapter. Thus, I want to start this book where the other book left off. Furthermore, I do my best to end this book in manner that will lead into the beginning of the last book. To which, it won't really matter which one you read first. But I digress.

When the bible says that the sons of Eli were worthless men, there is a different phrase used to describe them in the original Hebrew. In the Hebrew, the phrase used to describe Eli's sons was "Sons of Belial". Belial (běli-yaal) was a name meaning "Worthless", which is believed to be derived from the Hebrew words beli (without) and ya'al (to be of value). Some scholars translate Belial to "worthless" (beli yo'il) or to "yokeless" (Beli ol). No matter the translation, a son of Belial was a person marked by rebellion and unrestraint.

An ox that refused to be placed under a "yoke" would have been essentially worthless in the eyes of the Israelites. Furthermore, Exodus 21: 28-30 says the following: "If an ox gores a man or a woman to death, <u>the ox shall surely be stoned</u> and its flesh shall not be eaten; <u>but the owner of the ox shall go unpunished</u>. If, however, an ox <u>was previously in the habit of goring and its owner *has been* warned, yet he *does not* confine it</u> and it kills a man or a woman, the ox shall be stoned <u>and its owner also shall be put</u>

<u>to death</u>. If a ransom is demanded of him, then he shall give for the redemption of his life whatever is demanded of him."

This law helps to illustrate the issue with Eli and his sons. Eli's sons had a reputation for being unrestrained men and not "yoking" themselves to the Law of God. Furthermore, Eli knew about the behavior of his sons and even rebuked them for their behavior, himself. However, his sons continued to act wickedly, and he wouldn't remove them from their position. To which, God punishes them so that not only were Eli's sons killed for their behavior, but Eli died for his negligence, as well, just like a man who knows he has an ox with a dangerous reputation but does nothing about it at the peril of the people. Inasmuch, we shouldn't refrain from getting rid of worthless men and women in our midst, or else we shall bear the guilt and condemnation with them.

Why do I make this assertion? I do so, for even Paul wrote in 1 Corinthians 9: 8-10, concerning his right to ask for money, "I am not speaking these things according to human judgment, am I? Or does not the Law also say these things? For it is written in the Law of Moses, 'YOU SHALL NOT MUZZLE THE OX WHILE HE IS THRESHING.' <u>God is not concerned about oxen, is He</u>? Or is He speaking altogether for our sake? Yes, <u>for our sake it was written</u>, because the plowman ought to plow in hope, and the thresher to thresh in hope of sharing the crops."

Furthermore, Exodus 23: 4-5 says, "If you meet <u>your enemy's</u> ox or his donkey going astray, <u>you</u> shall bring it back to him. If you see the donkey <u>of one who hates you</u> lying down under its burden, <u>you</u> shall refrain from leaving him with it; <u>you</u> shall rescue it with him" (ESV). Thus, if you are to help your enemy's animal when it's wandering astray, how much more should you help your enemy when he goes astray? If we are to help a heavily burdened animal that belongs to someone who hates us, how much more so should we help those who hate us with their burdens? (As you can see, Jesus taught nothing new when He commanded us to love our enemies and to help them when they are in need.)

Why do I go into all this? I do so, for at the same time I was writing about the sons of Eli in my last book, a friend of mine and other Christians were in the process of exorcising demons from a woman who was involved with witchcraft for decades. They met up with her on multiple occasions and were doing all they could, but they were inexperienced when it came to exorcising demons. However, during the process, my friend was dealing with a specific demon on a certain occasion. When he asked for the demon to identify itself, he said Ellegua, but said its English name was Belial. When my friend asked Belial about his function and what right he claimed to have on the woman, Belial said he was the demon of false-doctrine. This information got me investigating, which led me to the conclusions I wrote prior to this paragraph, which I wrote for the sake of giving a foundation to the rest of what I'm about to write in the following paragraphs.

When speaking to the Pharisees, the Pharisees claimed to be children of Abraham for the sake of giving themselves credibility in the sight of the religious. However, Jesus said in John 8:44, "You are of your father the devil, and you want to do the desires of your father. He was a murderer from the beginning, and does not stand in the truth because there is no truth in him. Whenever he speaks a lie, he speaks from his own nature, for he is a liar and the father of lies." It is for this reason that I don't rely heavily on what my friend has told me about what he heard the demons say. I *do* trust him when he says, "this is what *they* said", but that doesn't mean that what they said was *trustworthy*, and even my friend proceeds with the same skepticism in mind.

However, the passage in John 8 highlights a specific point: The Pharisees were false teachers, teaching false doctrines, and were doing so while making grand gestures of piety and generosity for the sake of deceiving their followers into believing that what they taught (and the image they portrayed themselves as being) was legitimate. And when it comes to false teachers, whether before the Pharisees, or afterwards, the motive and method is the same. They want power, status, and wealth, and they twist, or even ignore, what God has said for the sake of achieving that goal. Even the serpent in the garden caused doubt by asking, "Did God really say?" and then misrepresented God and what He said to mean something else.

Before I go further, I want you to have this passage in mind: Deuteronomy 13: 1-5 says ,"If a prophet or a dreamer of dreams arises among you and gives you a sign or a wonder, and the sign or the wonder <u>comes *true*</u>, concerning which he spoke to you, saying, '<u>Let us go after *other gods* (whom you have not known) and let us serve *them*</u>,' you *shall not* listen to the words of that prophet or that dreamer of dreams; <u>for the LORD your God is *testing* you</u> to find out if you love the LORD your God with all your heart and with all your soul. You shall follow the LORD your God and fear Him; <u>and you shall keep His commandments [that which is written in the Law, prophets, and scripture]</u>, listen to His voice, serve Him, and cling to Him. <u>But that prophet or that dreamer of dreams *shall be put to death*, because he has counseled *rebellion* against the LORD your God</u> who brought you from the land of Egypt and redeemed you from the house of slavery, <u>to seduce you from the way in which the LORD your God commanded you to walk</u>. So, you shall purge the evil from among you."

In this passage, Israel is warned that not only will there be false prophets rising up among them, but that their false prophecies may even come *true*! But, how would they know if the man was a false prophet if his prophecies are coming true? Because he will tell them, "Let us go after other gods (whom you have not known) and let us serve them." Simply put, the false prophet will encourage the people to break the first commandment written

4

down in the Law. In other words, he will encourage them to do something that is contrary to that which has been previously written or spoken. Thus, you can know whether someone is a false teacher simply by how he treats the *full* Word of God.

Furthermore, Paul wrote in 2 Corinthians 6: 14-15, saying, "Do not be <u>unequally *yoked*</u> with unbelievers. For what partnership has righteousness with <u>lawlessness</u>? Or what fellowship has light with darkness? What accord has Christ with <u>Belial</u>? Or what portion does a believer share with an unbeliever?" Thus, whether it be the Old Testament or the New Testament, we are to have nothing to do with those who feel unrestrained by the fullness of Scripture. We are not to yoke ourselves with those who are yokeless.

There are 3 main types of false teachers today:

1) The Liberal Theologian

2) The Charismatic Celebrity

3) The Legalistic Pharisee

The Liberal Theologian is typically someone who questions the authority of Scripture altogether. That being, all of scripture is subjective to one's own values and beliefs. Such people affirm LGBTQ+ lifestyles, egalitarianism (no difference between gender roles), women pastors/overseers, pro-choice propaganda, communism, universalism (all paths lead to Heaven), Black Liberation Theology (White people can't go to heaven unless they sell everything they have and give the money to black people) and a few others.

The Charismatic Celebrity is a generalization of the private-jet flying, expensive car driving, mansion having, energetic faith healers you see on TV, not to mention their poorer but lifestyle affirming partners in crime who wish they were as popular and rich as the others. When I see such "pastors", I am reminded of the verse in Proverbs 29:18 which says, "Where there is no vision, the people are unrestrained, but happy is he who keeps the law." To which, I like to reverse the logic, in saying, "Where the people are unrestrained, there is no vision." In this case, *prophetic* vision.

What do I mean? I mean this: I don't care how many visions or prophecies these so-called preachers claim to have if they are completely unrestrained in their lifestyle or teaching. Furthermore, if the members of the church are unrestrained, especially if the pastor encourages the mayhem, then such pastors know nothing about what Paul meant when he said that God was not the author of confusion, i.e. mayhem and hysteria.

And lastly, the Legalistic Pharisee is the false teacher who adds to the word of God, especially to the law. That being, liberals and charismatics remove the restraints of scripture for the sake of their teachings, but legalists *add* to the restraints. Not only that, but they consider their traditions to overrule scripture, which such practices are seen in all kinds of churches and denominations.

Whether those false teachers are liberal, charismatic, legalistic, or some other so-called denomination, we are to take care when it comes to those who add to or take away from Scripture. However, before I get into the specifics, I will continue on the topic at hand.

No matter which of the three groups a false teacher falls into, if not a lesser fourth group, there is one thing in common: Scripture is not sufficient for them. Let us look at what Jesus Himself had to say of the Old Testament in Matthew 5: 17-19: "Do not think that I came to abolish the Law or the Prophets; I did not come to abolish but to fulfill. For truly I say to you, until heaven and earth pass away, not the smallest letter or stroke shall pass from the Law <u>until *all* is accomplished.</u> *Whoever* then annuls one of the least of these commandments, and teaches others to do the same, shall be called least in the kingdom of heaven; but whoever keeps and teaches them, he shall be called great in the kingdom of heaven."

The Law and the prophets were the summarization of what we now call the Old Testament. For Matthew 22: 37-40 also says, "And He said to him, "'YOU SHALL LOVE THE LORD YOUR GOD WITH ALL YOUR HEART, AND WITH ALL YOUR SOUL, AND WITH ALL YOUR MIND.' This is the great and foremost command-ment. The second is like it, 'YOU SHALL LOVE YOUR NEIGHBOR AS YOURSELF.' On these two commandments depend the whole <u>Law and the Prophets</u>."

However, the "Law" was a summarization of the first five books of the Old Testament. The first of those books was Genesis, which the events and instructions of Genesis predate Moses and the Law. Furthermore, the story of Job is believed to have existed before Moses as well, but Job isn't included in the "Law". Inasmuch, the "Law" that Jesus is referring to in Matthew isn't limited to the Law of Moses, also known as the Levitical Law that governed the theocratic state of Israel, but the *entirety* of what Moses and the other writers of the Old Testament wrote.

Jesus also said to the Pharisees in John 5: 39-47: "You search <u>the Scriptures</u> (the Law and the Prophets) because you think that in them you have eternal life; <u>it is these [Scriptures] that testify about *Me*</u>; and you are unwilling to come to Me so that you may have life. I do not receive glory from men; but I know you, that <u>you do not have the love of God in yourselves</u>. I have come in My Father's name, and you do not receive Me; if another comes in his own name, you will receive him. <u>How can you believe, when you receive glory from one another and you do not seek the glory that is from the one and only God?</u> Do not think that *I* will accuse you before the Father; the one who accuses you is *Moses*, in whom you have set your hope. For <u>if you believed *Moses*, you would believe *Me*, for he wrote about Me. But if you do not believe *his* writings, how will you believe *My* words</u>?"

If there was ever a time for Jesus to address the reliability of the Old Testament, it was during His time on earth. If there was ever a time to say, "Hey, that prophet got it wrong in this passage" or "You should stop reading that book altogether", it was then. The Hebrew Bible had already been canonized and translated into the Greek Septuagint over 100 years before Jesus came, and yet, He didn't tell the Pharisees they got it wrong. However, the Sadducees, who were liberal, only adhered to the Law (Genesis, Exodus, Leviticus, Numbers, and Deuteronomy) and ignored everything else. Nevertheless, Jesus never casted doubt on the accuracy of Scripture, or what should be counted as Scripture. Jesus only attacked the Pharisees' and Sadducees' understanding and teachings of Scripture.

Furthermore, Jesus told the Disciples (who, other than Judas, would become the Apostles) in John 15: 18-27: "<u>If the world hates you [the Apostles], you know that it has hated Me before it hated you</u>. If you were of the world, the world would love its own; but because you are not of the world, but I chose you out of the world, because of this the world hates you. Remember the word that I said to you, 'A slave is not greater than his master.' <u>If they persecuted *Me*, they will also persecute *you*; if they kept *My* word, they will keep *yours* also</u>. But all these things they will do to you for My name's sake, because they do not know the One who sent Me. If I had not come and spoken to them, they would not have sin, but now they have no excuse for their sin. He who hates Me hates My Father also. If I had not done among them the works which no one else did, they would not have sin; but now they have both seen and hated Me and My Father as well.

But they have done this to fulfill the word that is written in their Law, 'THEY HATED ME WITHOUT A CAUSE.'

When the Helper [the Holy Spirit] comes, whom I will send to you from the Father, that is the Spirit of truth who proceeds from the Father, He will testify about Me, and *you* [the Apostles] will testify also, because you have been with Me from the beginning."

Jesus told the Apostles that if the world listened to what He says of Himself, then the world would listen to what the Apostles say of Him. Not only that, but Jesus would send them the Spirit of truth, and the Apostles and the Spirit of truth would testify of Jesus, together.

Jesus also said in John 16: 7-15: "But I tell you the truth, it is to your advantage that I go away; for if I do not go away, the Helper will not come to you; but if I go, I will send Him to you. And He, when He comes, will convict the world concerning sin and righteousness and judgment; concerning sin, because they do not believe in Me; and concerning righteousness, because I go to the Father and you no longer see Me; and concerning judgment, because the ruler of this world has been judged.

I have many more things to say to you, *but you cannot bear them now*. But when He, the Spirit of truth, comes, He will guide you into *all the truth*; for He will not speak on *His own* initiative, but whatever He *hears*, He will speak; and He will disclose to you what is to come. He will glorify Me, for He will take of Mine and will disclose it to you. All things that the Father has are Mine; therefore, I said that He takes of Mine and will disclose it to you."

Thus, when the Apostles received the Holy Spirit at Pentecost, they did not merely receive power for the sake of healing and wonders, but they received the understanding of the fullness of Scripture. That being, they perfectly understood the Law, the prophets, and the teachings of Christ. The Holy Spirit *never* contradicts Scripture, but gives clarity to it. If the Holy Spirit were to ever contradict Scripture, He would be contradicting Jesus Himself. For Jesus said that the Holy Spirit does not speak on His own initiative, but speaks what He is told to speak. Thus, how can the Spirit say anything that contradicts Christ? If the Holy Spirit said something that contradicted Christ, and He only says what Christ tells Him to say, then Christ would have to contradict Himself. Thus, if Christ affirms the Old Testament Scriptures, Himself, and the Apostles, so does the Spirit.

Not only that, but Peter says in 2 Peter 3: 14-18: "Therefore, beloved, since you look for these things, be diligent to be found by Him in peace, spotless and blameless, and regard the patience of our Lord as salvation; just as also <u>our beloved brother *Paul*,</u> <u>according to the wisdom given him, wrote to *you*, as also in *all his*</u> *letters*, speaking in them of these things, in which are some things hard to understand, <u>which the *untaught and unstable distort*, as</u> <u>they do also *the rest of the Scriptures*, to their own destruction</u>. You therefore, beloved, knowing this beforehand, <u>be on your</u> <u>guard so that you are not carried away by the error of *unprinci-*</u> <u>*pled* men</u> and fall from your own steadfastness, but grow in the grace and knowledge of our Lord and Savior Jesus Christ. To Him be the glory, both now and to the day of eternity. Amen."

Thus, Peter not only affirms Paul a legitimate brother in the faith, but equates whatever he says as Scripture! For Peter didn't say, "as they do Scripture" but "the rest of the Scriptures". Simply put, Peter is saying that whatever Paul writes is to be counted as Scripture.

And what does Paul have to say about Himself? That *he* is an Apostle. Not only that, but in 1 Timothy 5:18, Paul says, "For the <u>Scripture</u> says, "YOU SHALL NOT MUZZLE THE OX WHILE HE IS THRESHING," *and* "<u>The laborer is worthy of his wages</u>." The phrase "the laborer is worthy of his wages", isn't mentioned in the Old Testament, but is only found written in Luke 10:7. Although the concept was mentioned in Leviticus 19:13 and Deuteronomy 24:14-15, the explicit phrase is only mentioned in Luke. Not only that, but the context of Luke 10:7 is Jesus giving the Disciples instructions as to how they are to conduct themselves while preaching the Gospel, making Paul's point more abundantly clear. And Paul says that the Scripture says "The laborer is worthy of his wages". Thus, Paul equates Luke's gospel as Scripture. Given that the Gospel of Luke and the Book of Acts were two parts of a single document, then the Book of Acts is to be counted as Scripture as well.

Furthermore, the Gospel of Mark is traditionally regarded as Peter's Gospel, and Mark was his scribe. Even if it wasn't Peter's Gospel, Paul speaks highly of Mark in his letters, although Paul doesn't necessarily say that whatever Mark writes is to be considered Scripture. Also, in fairness, Paul affirms Mark, Aristarchus, Demas, and Luke as fellow workers in Philemon 1:24, but would later condemn Demas in 2 Timothy.

For Paul writes Timothy in 2 Timothy 4: 9-11, saying, "Make every effort to come to me soon; for Demas, having loved this present world, has *deserted me* and gone to Thessalonica; Crescens has gone to Galatia, Titus to Dalmatia. Only Luke is with me. Pick up *Mark* and bring him with you, for he is useful to me for service." Granted, if whatever Paul writes is Scripture, and he called Demas a fellow worker in one letter, but called him a deserter in another, is Paul to be considered untrustworthy? Could Demas have deserted Paul in the same manner that Mark himself did in Acts 13:13? Even Paul refused to take Mark with him in Acts 15:38, "But Paul kept insisting that they should not take him along who had *deserted them* in Pamphylia and had not gone with them to the work." Who knows?

Mark is believed by many modern scholars to be the first gospel ever written, and the theory came about in the 19th century. Even if that were true, even if Mark's account wasn't Peter's, there would have been plenty of time before the writing of the other Gospels or the deaths of the Apostles to clear up any confusion. However, the tradition that says Mark is actually Peter's Gospel sheds doubt that Mark was the first gospel to be written [See citations for the link to the video]. The tradition says that Peter was giving a sermon in Rome about the life of Jesus, and Mark was hastily writing down what he was saying, as to why Mark heavily uses the phrase "immediately". For the phrase "immediately" in those times didn't necessarily mean "the very next thing that happened", as we use the phrase today, but "immediately" is also a way of saying "fast forward" or "skipping ahead".

Nevertheless, when Mark supposedly asked Peter if he wanted him to publish what he wrote down, Peter essentially said, "You can if you want," which Dr. David Alan Black argues that if there were no other gospel accounts before Mark, why wouldn't Peter be more enthusiastic about publishing his account? He says another church tradition says the two gospels with the genealogies were written first (Matthew and Luke). To which, everything about the Gospel of Mark's legitimacy is all traditional hearsay, not personally written down by the Apostles themselves.

Even so, no matter what position you take, I think Mark's Gospel should be considered reliable. Whether it had Peter's direct stamp of approval, or it wasn't directly rebuked by the Apostles after decades of circulation, it stands to reason that Mark should be counted as Scripture. If you don't think so, you still have the Gospels of Matthew and John, who were Apostles, the Gospel of Luke and the Book of Acts, of which the Apostle Paul affirms. You also have all of Paul's letters, both of Peter's letters, John's 3 letters and the book of Revelation. But what about James and Jude, the half-brothers of Jesus?

Luke writes in Acts 1: 13-14, saying, "When they had entered the city, they went up to the upper room where they were staying; that is, <u>Peter and John and James and Andrew, Philip and Thomas, Bartholomew and Matthew, James the son of Alphaeus, and Simon the Zealot, and Judas the son of James</u>. These all with one mind were continually devoting themselves to prayer, along with the women, and <u>Mary the mother of Jesus, and with *His brothers*</u>."

Later, in Acts 2: 1-4, Luke writes about the same group of people, saying, "When the day of Pentecost had come, <u>they were *all together*</u> <u>in one place</u>. And suddenly there came from heaven a noise like a violent rushing wind, and it filled the whole house where they were sitting. And there appeared to them tongues as of fire distributing themselves, and <u>they rested on *each one of them*</u>. And *they were all* <u>filled with the Holy Spirit and began to speak with other tongues, as the Spirit was giving *them* utterance</u>."

Thus, the same Holy Spirit that gave understanding to the Apostles came upon the brothers of Jesus, Mary, and even the women (possibly their wives) who were praying with them. For Paul writes in 1 Corinthians 9:5, "Do we not have a right to take along a believing wife, even as the rest of the apostles and <u>the brothers of the Lord</u> and Cephas?" Cephas was another name for Peter. Thus, Paul lumps the brothers of the Lord into the same group as he does the Apostles. It should stand to reason that anything they wrote should be counted as Scripture. Thus, James and Jude should be considered Scripture.

Lastly, what about the Book of Hebrews? The authorship of Hebrews is debated even amongst the greatest of scholars. Although there is nothing in the Book of Hebrews that contradicts the rest of Scripture, there isn't necessarily any Apostle who affirms it, either. That being said, I consider it to be Scripture, but what authority do I have?

All in all, even if you still doubt the reliability of Mark, Hebrews, James, and Jude, the other 23 writings of the New Testament still hold under scrutiny. If you want to cast doubt on what Jesus said about the legitimacy of the Apostles, given that everything we know about Jesus was written by the Apostles, then you might as well cast doubt on *everything* the Apostles said about Jesus. Thus, you should cast doubt on *everything* that Jesus said, which includes what He said about the Old Testament. Thus, you should cast doubt on *everything* the Bible says. To which, if you are to doubt *everything*, how can you trust *anything*?

Why even bother with the Bible? If it was written by men, and men are prone to error, why should we waste time with it? That being said, if we can't trust the writings and opinions of men 2,000 years ago, why should I trust the writings and opinions of anyone today? For even if the Apostles wrote their heartfelt opinions and trustworthy observances *today*, someone else will say 2,000 years from now "How can I trust any of this?"

Thus, if there is to be any objective authority, it has to come from outside of ourselves. For if *my* truth is as true as *your* truth, and those truths contradict one another, then how is it objective? Thus, if there is an objective authority figure out there, he, she, or it, would have to be greater than human. That being, God. And unless God speaks to us to let us know what He is like and what He expects of us, how could we possibly know anything about Him, Her, It, or some other preferred pronoun? Thus, if there is a God who has been made known to us, that God would have to be a God that is spoken of in one of the known religions. If the true God is an unknown God to the rest of the world (not mentioned in the existing religions) and you claim to know what the true God is like, then you make yourself out to be the God's prophet. To which, how can I know that anything *you* say about God is trustworthy? Thus, once again, if we can't trust a 2,000-year-old book, or any other written religion, why should we trust *you* in the present day?

However, there are plenty of people today who claim to be followers of Christ, some even claiming *Apostleship*, and yet, they do not yoke themselves to the authority of Scripture. Whenever you call them out on it, they say, "The Lord told me" or "the Holy Spirit told me". As mentioned, the Holy Spirit never contradicts Scripture, to which, as I argued, all of the Holy Bible is Scripture. Not only that, but many of these "children of Belial" will agree that the entirety of the Holy Bible is Scripture. However, they claim that whatever the "Spirit" says trumps whatever Scripture says. They claim that I should take their word for it, given that they are an Apostle or prophet. But how can I know that they are an Apostle or a prophet? They say, "God said I am."

But what does Paul, an Apostle of Christ Jesus, whose writings are to be counted as Scripture, say on the subject? 2 Corinthians 11: 12-15 says, "But what I am doing I will continue to do, so that I may cut off opportunity from those who desire an opportunity to be regarded just as we [the Apostles] are in the matter about which they are *boasting*. For such men are false apostles, deceitful workers, disguising themselves as apostles of Christ. No wonder, for even Satan disguises himself as an angel of light. Therefore, it is not surprising if his servants also disguise themselves as servants of righteousness, whose end will be according to their deeds."

Furthermore, Paul writes in Galatians 1: 8-9, saying, "But even if *we [the Apostles]*, or *an angel* from heaven, should preach to you a gospel contrary to what *we [the Apostles]* have preached to you, he is to be accursed! As we [the Apostles] have said before, so I say again now, if *any* man [in the present or future] is preaching to you a gospel *contrary* to what you received, he is to be accursed!" Paul is saying that if even he or the other Apostles were to contradict themselves and start preaching a new gospel, they should be accursed! If an angel, or the very writers of the Scriptures themselves, were to start teaching a different message, they should go to hell! Thus, how can anyone who claims to be an Apostle or a prophet teach another message or teaching contrary to what the Apostles taught and consider themselves an Apostle? Or even a Christian?

How? For these children of Belial say, "It wasn't an angel or an apostle who gave me this message, but the Holy Spirit, Himself." Again, the Holy Spirit *cannot* contradict Scripture, but only give clarity to it. However, someone I dealt briefly with quoted 2 Corinthians 3:17, which says, "Now the Lord is the Spirit, and where the Spirit of the Lord is, there is liberty." She was trying to convince me that the verse meant "The Spirit is free to do what He wants, even go against what is written."

Not only that, but there are those in the New Apostolic movement who teach the same thing, using the same verse. For the passage in 2 Corinthians also says in verses 4-6 "Such confidence we have through Christ toward God. Not that we are adequate in ourselves to consider anything as coming from ourselves, but our adequacy is from God, who also made us adequate as servants of *a new covenant*, not of *the letter* but of the Spirit; for *the letter* kills, but the Spirit gives life." These so-called apostles say "the letter" being referred to in this passage is talking about the entirety of Scripture itself! Meaning, Scripture kills, but the Spirit gives life. Meaning, we must rely on what the Spirit tells us, not Scripture.

Again, and again I say, again, the Spirit can never contradict Scripture, but only give clarity to it. Furthermore, if you read the entirety of the passage, "the letter" that Paul is referring to is the Levitical Law of Moses! For the entire chapter says this:

"Are we beginning to commend ourselves again? Or do we need, as some, letters of commendation to you or from you? You are our letter, written in our hearts, known and read by all men; being manifested that you are a letter of Christ, cared for by us, written not with ink but with the Spirit of the living God, <u>not on tablets of stone</u> but on tablets of human hearts.

Such confidence we have through Christ toward God. Not that we are adequate in ourselves to consider anything as coming from ourselves, but our adequacy is from God, who also made us adequate as servants of a new covenant, <u>not of the letter</u> but of the Spirit; <u>for the letter kills</u>, but the Spirit gives life.

<u>But if *the ministry of death, in letters engraved on stones*, came with glory, *so that the sons of Israel* could not look intently at the face of *Moses* because of the glory of his face, fading as it was</u>, how will the ministry of the Spirit fail to be *even more* with glory? <u>For if *the ministry of condemnation* has glory</u>, much more does the ministry of righteousness abound in glory. For indeed *what had* glory, in this case has no glory because of the glory that surpasses it. For if that which fades away was with glory, much more that which remains is in glory.

Therefore, having such a hope, we use great boldness in our speech, <u>and are not like Moses</u>, who used to put a veil over his face so that the sons of Israel would not look intently at the end of what was fading away. <u>But their minds were hardened; for until this very day at *the reading of the old covenant* the same veil remains unlifted</u>, because it is removed in Christ. But <u>to this day whenever Moses is read, a veil lies over their heart</u>; but whenever a person turns to the Lord, the veil is taken away. Now the Lord is the Spirit, and where the Spirit of the Lord is, there is liberty. But we all, with unveiled face, beholding as in a mirror the glory of the Lord, are being transformed into the same image from glory to glory, just as from the Lord, the Spirit."

The case that Paul is making in this passage isn't that the Spirit is free to contradict Scripture, nor that we are to ignore Scripture. He is saying that those who are still holding to the Old Covenant (that being, the Old Testament) while rejecting the New Covenant (that being, Jesus Christ and the message of the Apostles) are living under a curse. Paul is affirming what Jesus said in John when He said, "If they persecuted *Me*, they will also persecute *you*; if they kept *My* word, they will keep *yours* also. But all these things they will do to you for My name's sake, because <u>they do not know the One who sent Me</u>." Thus, Jesus is saying the reason the world and the Jews (for the most part) resist the gospel is because they resist God, Himself. The Jews practiced their religious activities and read the Old Testament, but none of it was being taken to heart.

Even so, Acts 17: 10-12 says, "The brethren immediately sent Paul and Silas away by night to Berea, and when they arrived, they went into <u>the synagogue of the Jews</u>. Now these were more noble-minded than those in Thessalonica, <u>for they received the word with great eagerness, *examining the Scriptures daily* to see whether these things were so. Therefore, many of them believed</u>, along with a number of prominent Greek women and men."

Paul speaks this new message, this new covenant, to the Jews in Berea, and by comparing what he was saying to them with the Old Testament, many of them believed unto salvation, and some Greeks believed as well. If the reading of Scripture kills, how can this be so? Yes, we must be born again by the Spirit, but salvation is never divorced from Scripture.

For Paul writes in Romans 10: 11-17: "For the Scripture says, 'WHOEVER BELIEVES IN HIM WILL NOT BE DISAPPOINTED.' For there is no distinction between Jew and Greek; for the same Lord is Lord of all, abounding in riches for all who call on Him; for 'WHOEVER WILL CALL ON THE NAME OF THE LORD WILL BE

SAVED.' <u>How then will they call on Him in whom they have not believed? How will they believe in Him</u> *whom they have not heard*<u>? And how will they hear</u> *without a preacher*<u>? How will they preach</u> *unless they are sent*? Just as it is written, 'HOW BEAUTIFUL ARE THE FEET OF THOSE WHO BRING GOOD NEWS OF GOOD THINGS!' However, they did not all heed the good news; for Isaiah says, 'LORD, WHO HAS BELIEVED OUR REPORT?' <u>So, faith comes from hearing, and hearing</u> *by the word of Christ*."

I shall wrap up the point of this chapter with Paul's writing to Timothy in 2 Timothy 3: 12-17, "Indeed, all who desire to live godly in Christ Jesus will be persecuted. <u>But evil men and impostors will proceed from bad to worse,</u> *deceiving and being deceived*. You, however, continue in the things you have learned and become convinced of, knowing from whom you have learned them, and that from childhood you have known *the sacred writings* <u>which are able to give you the wisdom that leads to salvation through faith</u> which is in Christ Jesus. *All Scripture* <u>is inspired by God and profitable for teaching, for reproof, for correction, for training in righteousness; so that the man of God may be adequate, equipped for</u> *every good work*."

Yes, it's true, in that Scripture doesn't guide you as to where to work, who you should marry, whether or not you should get married, etc. However, the Spirit will never guide you to go against what Scripture has clearly written. The Spirit of truth and Scripture are inseparable. Salvation is inseparable from the Spirit and Scripture. Sanctification is inseparable from the Spirit and Scripture. Thus, you must ask yourself "Am I a Berean, or a Belial?"

CHARISMATICS VS CESSATIONISTS
(PART ONE)

1 Corinthians 14: 37-38: "If *anyone* [in the present or future] thinks he is a prophet or spiritual, let him recognize that <u>the things which I write to you are the *Lord's* commandment</u>. But if *anyone* [in the present or future] does not recognize this, <u>*he* is not recognized</u>."

Do you know what is great about that verse? Paul writes that verse in the context of telling the Corinthians how the gifts and callings of the Holy Spirit are to properly function. In the next few chapters, I will break down 1 Corinthians 12-14. For these chapters in 1 Corinthians are not only the basis upon which Charismatics justify being Charismatics, but also the basis upon which Cessationists justify being Cessationists. To which you may be asking: What is a Charismatic? What is a Cessationist?

Charismatics are those who not only believe that all the gifts of the Spirit are functioning today, (such as performing miracles, healings, prophesying, and speaking in tongues) but that those gifts are functioning in the same depth and manner today as they were in the time of the Apostles. I do not wish to attack *every* false teaching that is taught in Charismatic circles, for I would have to write a library's worth of books. I am simply going to write about what these three chapters teach about the gifts of the Holy Spirit and let Charismatics see where their teachings fall short.

Cessationists are those who think that the gifts of performing miracles, healings, prophecy, and speaking in tongues, are no longer operating today. Furthermore, they claim those types of gifts ended at the end of the Apostolic age (when the last Apostle died, essentially). Contrary to the accusations from the Charismatics, Cessationists *do not* teach that *all* the gifts of the Holy Spirit have ended, nor do they think miracles and healings *never* take place anymore. They do believe that some of the gifts are still in full operation (teachers, administrators, and such). They also believe God *does* perform miracles and heals people today. The difference is, they believe that such actions only happen through prayer and God's willingness to do so, not that a man or woman can make such actions happen on their own. Also, they believe that God doesn't speak in an audible voice to anyone anymore.

Before we get started, I want to say that I hold to neither of these teachings. That being, I do not believe all the gifts of the Holy Spirit are operating today in the same capacity (if not greater) than they were during the time of the Apostles. Yet, I do not believe the gifts have ended to the degree that Cessationists claim. For I have experienced enough experiences within myself to not become a Cessationist. If you haven't read *No Filter*, my personal testimony is that I tried to drown myself in a pool when I was in middle school, and God not only spoke to me in a soft voice to not go through with it, but He gave me a change of heart as well.

Furthermore, years later, when I was 21, I decided to get rebaptized, to which I started being harassed by demons at night. I would see dark figures in the room that didn't match any object or shadow that would normally be there. I would sometimes have my voice taken away, would be unable to move or breath until I mustered the ability to say the name of Jesus, and a few other things. Granted, *most* of these experiences were actually *dreams* where I was in my room and these things were happening, but there were plenty of times where there is no doubt in my mind that I was awake.

However, a week into the demonic *oppression* (not possession), God spoke to me in a dream where He essentially said, "Don't be afraid. However, if you're going to start receiving revelations from Me, you're also going to have visitations from demons." Although the demonic oppression and divine revelations were frequent in those first few months, they became less frequent over time. I also learned during that time that there is a difference between God speaking to someone in a dream and having a dream where God spoke to them. The first is from God, the second is from demons, the subconscious, food, or something else other than God. I have had plenty of both.

Nevertheless, of the dreams that I'm certain were from God, He was *never* telling me something that was contrary to Scripture. In fact, I would always search Scripture to see if there was a passage that backed it up. If God wasn't shedding light on a Scriptural truth that I never realized before, He was simply giving me a word of encouragement or direction. That being, if I was feeling depressed, He would tell me to cheer up. When it came to direction, it was simple things like "Quit your job" or "Don't quit your job" or "Don't pursue that woman". (In the case of that particular woman, she started going to a different church a few weeks after the dream, and soon after that she met the man who is now her husband.)

Having said all this, there is something I need to make clear: I am *NOT* able to make God give me a revelation. In fact, a year or so into receiving revelations, God told me, "I will only ever tell you what you need to know and when you need to know it". Also, as I grow in Scripture, sanctification, and conquering the issues within myself that I spoke of in *No Filter*, the dreams and visions become *less* frequent, not more. You would think that as I grow

23

in godliness the dreams would be even more frequent and more spectacular, but no.

Why? Because as I grow in godliness (reading the Bible, putting sin to death, and everything else that comes with spiritual growth) the less dependent I am on revelations. If you are saturating yourself with Scripture, you don't need an audible voice to tell you whether a church is basing their teachings on Scripture. The more you grow in yourself and knowing what to look for in a future spouse, the less you need any revelation to tell you whether or not dating and marrying a certain person is a good idea.

Even a certain false teacher from a certain church movement unknowingly backs up my claim. For Joel 2:28 says, "It will come about after this that I will pour out My Spirit on all mankind; and your sons and daughters will prophesy, your old men will dream dreams, your young men will see visions." This man teaches that visions are more literal and dreams are metaphorical and symbolic. He also teaches that "old men and young men" isn't necessarily talking about age, but spiritual maturity. Thus, when you're spiritually immature, you need visions, but when you mature, you receive dreams. To which, in this case, I would agree, in that as you mature in faith, the less dependent you have to be on the miraculous.

Having said that, this man also has a school where he claims you can be *taught* to prophesy, speak in tongues, and to perform the miraculous. How does that make any sense? On the one hand, he teaches that as you mature in your faith, the less audible and clear God will speak to you. On the other hand, the whole purpose of his school and teaching is to make it so you can receive prophetic words, speak in tongues, and perform miracles, at *your own* will. Where does he get this from? Unfortunately, he is amongst those who teach what I talked about in the last chapter. That being, "The letter kills, but the Spirit gives life." He is amongst those who teach that if the Spirit and Scripture contradict each other, we listen to the Spirit.

This man says in one of his books "Those who feel safe because of their intellectual grasp of Scriptures enjoy a false sense of security. None of us has a full grasp of Scripture, but we all have the Holy Spirit. He is our common denominator who will always lead us into truth. <u>But to follow Him, *we must be willing to follow off the map*-to go beyond what we know*.*"</u>

It is to that end that I don't lump all Charismatics into one group. For there are plenty within Charismatic circles who reject such a teaching. However, Charismatics tend to hold to many other beliefs that they think are Scripturally based, but are indeed, not. Because of which, almost *all* of my favorite preachers and teachers are Cessationists. For although I disagree with them on Cessationism, there is virtually nothing else that I disagree with when it comes the Scripture and spiritual matters. There is only one "Charismatic" preacher that I am willing to listen to, and a few "open-minded but cautious" preachers that I listen to. Even so, I must be careful to examine what is being taught.

You may be thinking, "Aren't you splitting hairs, here? Didn't you say that God told you to not pursue that woman, which would have been something 'outside of the map' of what we know in Scripture?" To a degree, yes. However, being told to not pursue a Christian woman simply because she didn't fit into God's specific plan for my life is far different than saying, for example, "God told me to divorce my wife and marry this other woman." For such a "revelation" would go against 1 Corinthians 7: 10-11 "But to the married I give instructions, not I, <u>but the *Lord*</u>, that the wife <u>should not leave</u> her husband (<u>but if she does leave, she *must remain unmarried*, or else be reconciled to her husband</u>), and that the husband <u>should not divorce</u> his wife."

Not that this man made such a claim and divorced his wife, but there are many people within Charismatic circles, pastors and non-pastors, who claim that God told them to leave their wife for another woman, or to break up another man's marriage and marry him. Typically, they don't have anything to go on to justify themselves, other than "The Lord told me". And if they justify it at all, they point to the false interpretation of "the letter kills, but the Spirit gives life" and "Where the Spirit is, there is freedom". I have also heard that passage used to justify women being pastors, which Scripture clearly forbids, but we will get into that later.

Nevertheless, he is right that the Holy Spirit always leads us into truth. However, as mentioned, the Spirit *never* contradicts Scripture. Thus, <u>even if</u> "the Spirit" gave you a new teaching, it will not negate an already existing teaching, just as bricks being added to a house don't negate the foundation and previous bricks. However, as with women pastors and other heresies, the whole "God told me" narrative is used to remove the yoke of Scripture to justify their teachings and behavior. If you love God and Scripture, you will reject such people and their teachings, whether you're a Charismatic, a Cessationist, or anywhere in between. Now, let's dig into 1 Corinthians 12-14:

1 Corinthians 12: 1-3 says, "Now concerning spiritual gifts, brethren, I do not want you to be unaware. You know that when you were pagans, you were led astray to the mute idols, however you were led. Therefore, <u>I make known to you that *no one* [in the present or future] speaking by the Spirit of God says, 'Jesus is accursed'; and *no one* [in the present or future] can say, 'Jesus is Lord,' except by the Holy Spirit</u>."

Surely no one in the Charismatic movement is saying, "Jesus is accursed", right? Maybe not directly, but indirectly. That being, they don't say that Jesus is accursed, but they say that one of His teachings is accursed. One such "woman pastor" said, "Anyone who tells you to deny yourself is of Satan!" She used this to justify the health, wealth, and prosperity gospel that she preaches, a "gospel" I adamantly reject in *No Filter*. Thus, she is saying that God wants us to be happy and enjoy the material things of the world.

However, Matthew 16: 24-26 says, "Then Jesus said to His disciples, "If *anyone* [in the present or future] wishes to come after Me, he [or she] *must deny* himself [or herself], and take up his [or her] *cross* and follow Me. For whoever wishes to save his [or her] life will lose it; but whoever loses his [or her] life for My sake will find it. For what will it profit a man [or woman] if he [or she] gains the whole world and forfeits his [or her] soul? Or what will a man [or woman] give in exchange for his [or her] soul?"

Denying your own desires and taking up a painful cross in pursuit of Christ wherever He leads doesn't look like a life in which Jesus' primary concern is your material/earthly happiness. Thus, how can such a woman, or any man who agrees with her, say *by the Spirit* "Jesus is accursed"? How can anyone, man or woman, *by the Spirit*, condemn or negate any part of Scripture? Moving on.

1 Corinthians 12: 4-11 says, "Now there are varieties of gifts, but the same Spirit. And there are varieties of ministries, and the same Lord. There are varieties of effects, but the same God who works all things in all persons. But to each one is given the manifestation of the Spirit *for the common good*. For to one is given the word of wisdom through the Spirit, and to another the word of knowledge according to the same Spirit; to another faith by the same Spirit, and to another gifts of healing by the one Spirit, and to another the effecting of miracles, and to another prophecy, and to another the distinguishing of spirits, to another various kinds of tongues, and to another the interpretation of tongues. But one and the same Spirit works all these things, distributing to each one individually just as *He* wills."

One of the arguments Cessationists make against Charismatics goes something like this: Someone with the gift of teaching or administration can exercise that gift at will. Therefore, those who claim to perform healings should be able to perform them at will. If there are those today with a legitimate gift of healing, then their ability to heal someone isn't dependent on the other person's faith. But if they do in fact have the gift of healing, then they are evil for not healing every person they come in contact with.

Let's break down the logic of that argument. "Teaching and administration is exercised at will. Therefore, miracles must be performed at will." Why make such a conclusion, given that 2 Peter 1: 20-21 says, "knowing this first of all, that no prophecy of Scripture comes from someone's own interpretation. For no prophecy was ever produced by the will of man, but men spoke from God as they were carried along by the Holy Spirit." (ESV) If prophecy isn't a matter of human will, then why is the gift of healing automatically assumed to be an act of the will simply because teaching and administration is an act of the will? I'm not defending the teachings and actions of notorious "faith healers" who prey on the desperate and gullible; I'm affirming what verses 4-11 say. That being, there are a variety of gifts, ministries, and effects.

However, I agree to the Cessationist argument of "whether or not someone gets healed isn't a matter of a lack of faith." For there are plenty of nonbelievers who get healed through natural medical methods, whereas there are plenty of believers who refuse to go to a doctor, saying, "I'm waiting for a miracle." There are many reasons why a miracle may not take place, although a lack of faith could indeed be the reason for some people. However, in the case of Pharoah, the supernatural plagues came upon him because of his lack of faith. And such is the case with many men and women in the Bible.

A relative of mine didn't believe a big-named Charismatic healer could heal her of a certain medical condition. She believed that healing was possible, but she thought the man was a joke. But when he was passing through her area in Texas, her friends begged her to go see him. She went to see him thinking "what can it hurt?" When she got up on the stage, he was laying hands on people so they fell over. Afraid of falling, she guarded herself and kept saying "I'm not going to fall over! I'm not going to fall over!"

Do you know what happened when he touched her? Nothing! She wasn't healed, she didn't fall over, nothing! He tried again, and still nothing! He got upset and moved on to the next person. She later got a letter in the mail from his ministry team asking her to write her testimony about how she was healed. She laughed thinking "These people must be pretty sure of themselves. They just don't quit." And guess what? She was healed the next morning. Does this prove that he was truly a man of God? No. However, it does go to show that her faith had nothing to do with whether or not she was healed. Yet, he, and others, claim that God can't heal someone who lacks faith.

And to the last part of the Cessationist argument: "any healer, who can heal at will, that doesn't heal every person possible, is evil." Did Jesus heal every single person possible? No. Is Jesus evil? No. However, whether or not the gift of healing is a matter of the will, the gift of teaching *is* a matter of the will. Yes, you need the Holy Spirit to guide you in discerning what Scripture says, but a teacher who is asked a question can give an answer without praying, fasting, etc. Yet, if we use the Cessationist logic against healers, we can also use it against teachers. That being, "any *teacher* that doesn't *teach* every person they possibly can is evil". Did Jesus teach every person possible? No. Is Jesus evil? No. However, the judgement in which we judge others will be judged unto ourselves. So, don't be so quick to judge someone as *evil*

29

simply because what they're doing doesn't make sense to *you*, when you do plenty of things that make no sense *at all*.

Nevertheless, 1 Corinthians 12:11 says regarding the gifts of the Spirit, "But one and the same Spirit works all these things, distributing to each one individually just as *He* wills." Meaning, *no one* has the ability to exercise *every* gift. Furthermore, *no one* can be *taught* how to gain a gift, much less *all* the gifts.

For 1 Corinthians 12: 12-26 says, "Or even as the body is one and yet has many members, and all the members of the body, though they are many, are one body, so also is Christ. For by one Spirit, we were all baptized into one body, whether Jews or Greeks, whether slaves or free, and we were all made to drink of one Spirit.

For the body is not one member, but many. If the foot says, 'Because I am not a hand, I am not a part of the body,' it is not for this reason any the less a part of the body. And if the ear says, 'Because I am not an eye, I am not a part of the body,' it is not for this reason any the less a part of the body. If the whole body were an eye, where would the hearing be? If the whole were hearing, where would the sense of smell be? But now God has placed the members, each one of them, in the body, *just as He desired*. If they were all one member, where would the body be? But now *there are many members, but one body*. And the eye cannot say to the hand, 'I have no need of you'; or again the head to the feet, 'I have no need of you.' On the contrary, it is much truer that the members of the body which seem to be weaker are necessary; and those members of the body which we deem less honorable, on these we bestow *more abundant honor*, and our less presentable members become much more presentable, whereas our more presentable members have no need of it. But God has so composed the body, giving more abundant honor to that member which lacked, *so that there may be no division in the body*, but that the members may have the same care for one another. And *if one member suffers, all the members suffer with it*; if one member is honored, all the members rejoice with it."

Paul is saying that even though the church is one body, it has different members that provide different functions for the good of the whole body. Not only that, but Paul argues that God did this on purpose so the whole body would have to work together for the sake of fulfilling the needs of the church. God did this so no one could say, "I have no need for the rest of the body (that is, the people of God), for I can do everything myself!" If every individual within the church had the ability to exercise every gift to the highest capacity and the widest effects, then there would be no need for the church to work together as a body, for everyone would be a one-man army.

Furthermore, Paul argues that the less desirable parts of the body (that being, the people with the less desirable gifts) are given more honor than those who possess the more desirable gifts. How is that so? I think of the story of the widow who gave the two copper coins, whereas the rich were giving their spare change. Jesus said of the widow "She gave more than all the rest, and will have a greater reward." The Apostles were greatly empowered by God, as to why they accomplished so much for the Kingdom of God, as far as what the human eye can see. However, those who are not incredibly gifted who perform their gifts in secret to the best of their ability have greater honor than that of the Apostles in the eyes of God.

I believe that is what Jesus meant when He said in John 14:12 "Truly, truly I say to you, the one who believes in Me, the works that I do, he will do also; and *greater works* than these he will do; because I am going to the Father." Jesus wasn't speaking of greater works in the sense of more spectacular, for what greater work can be done than being spiritually born again? To which, being born again is a work of the Holy Spirit, not a work of man. Also, Jesus wasn't speaking of greater works in the sense of the number of works performed, for who has ever performed more works than Jesus?

So how is it possible for the works to be greater than the works of Jesus? Jesus explained it when He said, "because I am going to the Father". Meaning, the works are greater because we are doing them for a God whom we cannot see. It's easy to do a job when the boss is right next to you, but to do your job when the boss isn't around is what makes you a great employee. Before Jesus told them about how they and others would do greater works than Himself, Jesus told the disciples that the Father was in Him and He was in the Father, and the Father did His work through Jesus. He also said that if they didn't believe that He and the Father were one, then they should believe because of the works themselves. Basically, Jesus is telling them, "If you don't believe what you are *hearing*, then believe because of what you have *seen*. If My *words* aren't enough for you to believe, then My *works* should be enough."

That is why the works will be greater than the works of Jesus. For if He goes to the Father, they (and we) will not be able to see the Father, Jesus, or the works that Jesus was performing on the earth. That being, the Apostles and the church would be performing their works through believing in what they can no longer see or had *never* seen. For we live by faith, not by sight. However, faith comes through hearing, and hearing through the word of God. Jesus knew what He knew and did what He did because He and the Father were one within the all-seeing Godhead from all eternity. The church does what it does through having faith in that unseen reality and the empowerment of the unseen Holy Spirit, despite our earthly limitations, a fact that Jesus mentions directly after He tells them about how they will perform greater works than Himself.

Furthermore, Jesus later said in John 20:29, "Because you have seen Me, have you now believed? <u>Blessed are they who did not see, and yet believed</u>." Inasmuch, the Apostles saw Jesus and His works, the early church saw the Apostles and their works, the later church only knew of the Apostles through letters they had written and witnessed the works of the church, etc. Today, virtually all we have to go on about God is what was preserved in Scripture. If we continue to do the works of Jesus in the belief that Scripture is true, then it's a greater work than that of Jesus or the Apostles. For we will be doing those works through faith in what the Scriptures tell us, not what we have seen with our own eyes.

Why is it that so many Charismatics believe that the Kingdom of Heaven is the performing of miracles? That being, why do they believe the power of God is most apparent when miracles are being performed? If such is the case, then why does Paul say in 1 Corinthians 2: 1-5, "And I, when I came to you, brothers, did not come proclaiming to you the testimony of God with lofty speech or wisdom. For <u>I decided to know nothing among you except Jesus Christ and Him crucified</u>. And I was with you in *weakness* and in *fear* and much *trembling*, and my speech and my message were not in plausible words of wisdom, but in demonstration of the Spirit and of power, <u>so that your faith might not rest in the wisdom of men-but in the power of God</u>." (ESV)

When Paul first arrived in Corinth, he didn't come with great philosophical arguments, nor did he perform miracles (or else, he would have made something known other than Christ and Him crucified). He did nothing except preach Jesus and the cross, for he did not want their faith to be dependent on clever arguments or signs and wonders. Not only that, but he spoke with weakness, not power. With trembling, not boldness. And yet, many came to believe in the message simply through the power of God within the message. Is that to say there isn't a place for the miraculous anymore, as the Cessationists claim? No, or else, why would Paul later give instructions to the Corinthians as to how the gifts of the Spirit are to be exercised?

Which begs the question: What is the Kingdom of God/Heaven? As mentioned, Charismatics often claim that the Kingdom of Heaven is the performing of miracles. But why? They say, "Because Jesus told us to pray 'Your kingdom come, Your will be done, <u>on earth as it is in heaven</u>.' There is no sickness in *heaven*, therefore, there should be no sickness on *earth*." How strange... Do you know what else isn't in heaven? Marriage. Are we therefore supposed to get divorced or abstain from marriage for the sake of making earth look like heaven? Of course, not.

Furthermore, John 2: 23-25 says, "Now when He was in Jerusalem at the Passover, during the feast, <u>many believed in His name as they observed His *signs* which He was doing</u>. But Jesus, on His part, was not entrusting Himself to them, because He knew all people, and because He did not need anyone to testify about mankind, for He Himself knew what was in mankind." To which, this story leads into John chapter 3. Now, when a passage starts with the phrase "Now", it is an expression meaning "Next story" or "change of subject". Some translations have John 3 start with "Now" and others do not. However, in the original Greek, there is indeed a "Now". However, given the placement and subject matter of chapter 3, I don't think it to be coincidental that what John writes in Chapter 3 comes after Chapter 2.

For John 3: 1-3 says, "Now there was a man of the Pharisees, named Nicodemus, a ruler of the Jews; this man came to Jesus at night [possibly the night of John 2] and said to Him, 'Rabbi, we know that You have come from God as a teacher; <u>for no one can do these *signs*</u> that You do unless God is with him.' Jesus responded and said to him, 'Truly, truly, I say to you, <u>unless someone is born again, he cannot *see* the kingdom of God.</u>'"

How could Jesus say that? If the Kingdom of God (or Heaven) is the performing of miracles, then Nicodemus has *already* seen it! But Jesus said that unless he is born again, he cannot see the Kingdom of God. To which, seeing miracles alone isn't enough to be born again. Hearing clever arguments aren't enough to be born again. Being born again and coming to faith in Jesus Christ is a work of the Holy Spirit through the preaching of the gospel, and *nothing* else! So, what did Jesus mean when He said to pray, "Your kingdom come, Your will be done, on earth as it is in heaven"?

Charismatics emphasize the phrase "On earth as it is in heaven", but I believe the key is "Your will be done". For let's put it this way "Your kingdom come, Your *will* be done, on earth as it is in heaven". For after Jesus gives a teaching about the *exorcising of demons*, Luke 11: 27-29 says, "While Jesus was saying these things, one of the women in the crowd raised her voice and said to Him, 'Blessed is the womb that carried You, and the breasts at which You nursed!' But He said, 'On the contrary, blessed are those who hear the word of God and follow it.' Now as the crowds were increasing, He began to say, 'This generation is a wicked generation; it demands a *sign*, and so no sign will be given to it except the sign of Jonah.'"

This woman is amazed after hearing about demons and thinks "This is the coolest thing ever! Jesus is the man! His mother should be so proud of herself for raising such a demon expert!" However, Jesus rebukes her, saying, "It is better to hear the word of God and follow it." Let's put it this way: Jesus said, "Many will say to Me on that day, 'Lord, Lord! Did I not cast out demons in the name of Jesus?!' And I will say to them, 'Why do you call Me Lord if you don't do what I say?'" As to why I say the Kingdom of God isn't the performing of miracles, healing, prophesying, speaking in tongues, or casting out demons, but obedience to the word of God. The Kingdom of Heaven is mankind obeying the instruction of the Lord to the degree that the angels of Heaven obey. Some serve one purpose, some another, but all obey the word of God and perform their tasks. To which, the church, Christ's body, is to function the same way.

As to why the rest of 1 Corinthians 12: 27-31 says, "Now you are Christ's body, and individually members of it. And God has appointed in the church, *first* apostles, *second* prophets, *third* teachers, *then* miracles, *then* gifts of healings, helps, administrations, various kinds of tongues. All are not apostles, are they? All are not prophets, are they? All are not teachers, are they? All are not workers of miracles, are they? All do not have gifts of healings, do they? All do not speak with tongues, do they? All do not interpret, do they? But earnestly desire the greater gifts. And I show you a still more excellent way."

It is to that end that I reject any teaching that says that the Kingdom of God is solely the performing of the supernatural. It is also why I reject any teaching that says that Christians should have *all* the gifts of the Spirit. It is why I reject any teaching that says you can be taught how to gain the gifts of the Spirit. Not that you can't be taught how to increase in a gift that you already have, but to gain a gift that the Holy Spirit didn't give you according to His own purpose. For Paul not only says it's acceptable to desire and pray to have gifts, but he even encourages them to do so. However, if there was a way to unlock every single gift, you would think that Paul or one of the other Apostles would have given that information.

So, why am I not a Cessationist after recognizing such abuses and false-teachings from the Charismatic movements? Do you notice the ordering of the gifts? There are apostles, prophets, teachers, miracles, healing, helps, administrations, and tongues. Cessationists get rid of Apostles and prophets, keep teachers, get rid of miracles and healing, keep helps and administrations, and get rid of tongues. Why some and not the others? Do

Cessationists forsake such gifts because they can't organize such gifts in a systematic manner as they do theology? Are they not much different from the Atheists, in that they are only willing to believe in what they can see and write down into a formula? Is it merely a knee-jerk reaction to the abuses and abominations coming out of Charismatic movements? Could it be because they can't understand how someone with *their expertise* in theology wouldn't be given the more supernatural gifts as well, if they indeed still existed? Who knows?

If Cessationists will not believe my own testimony, then they should believe what Paul writes. To which, of course, they claim to do. Not only that, but the greatest argument that Cessationists have for their beliefs is later at the end of 1 Corinthians 13. To which, we will get into that at the end of the next chapter.

CHARISMATICS VS CESSATIONISTS (PART TWO)

1 Corinthians 13: 1-3: "If I speak with the tongues of mankind and of angels, but do not have love, I have become a noisy gong or a clanging cymbal. If I have the gift of prophecy and know all mysteries and all knowledge, and if I have all faith so as to remove mountains, but do not have love, I am nothing. And if I give away all my possessions to charity, and if I surrender my body so that I may glory, but do not have love, it does me no good."

One of the things I often notice when it comes to many faith healers and teachers is their lack of love for their enemies. And by enemies, I mean critics. Whenever certain faith healers are questioned upon their methods or theology, they often rebuke the critic as a blasphemer of the Holy Spirit, rather than give a biblical defense for their methods. Why? Because they typically don't have one. As mentioned, many justify themselves by claiming to have a special revelation from God Himself. Thus, for anyone to rebuke them is to rebuke God. However, God can't contradict God, Scripture can't contradict God, and God can't contradict Scripture.

Yet, this passage in 1 Corinthians demonstrates for us that love is a superior calling than any gift of the Spirit. For even if you do in fact speak in tongues or prophesy, if you do not have love, you are nothing. Many will say to Jesus on the day of judgement, "Lord,

Lord! Did we not prophesy, work miracles, or cast out demons in Your name?" And Jesus will say to them, "Why do you call Me Lord but don't do what I say?" If the greatest commandments are to love God and others, how are you being obedient to Christ when you accuse everyone to be an enemy of the cross whenever someone doesn't think exactly as you do? To which, even if you actually speak in tongues or prophesy, your credibility is heavily tarnished.

However, Paul also writes in this passage that even if you gave away all your possessions and died as a martyr, if you don't have love, there is no reward for what you've done. Yet, many leaders in these Charismatic circles aren't giving away their possessions, but acquiring and hoarding them. They don't risk their lives for the gospel on the frontlines of the spiritual battlefields, but stand behind a pulpit surrounded by security guards in a country protected by freedom of speech.

False apostles never pave the way for the gospel, but drive their cars down the roads the true apostles paved with their own blood. The false apostles boast in their rights as a minister of God, whereas Paul refused those rights for the sake of giving his ministry greater credibility. I once saw a parking spot while driving through a town that said "Reserved for Apostle [Man's Name]". I'm not saying that Paul wouldn't have a car, nor would he necessarily rebuke the notion of having his own parking spot, but I know Paul well enough to know he would have done something different if it was a stumbling block for others. Why? Because his main concern was loving God and others; to be a minister of peace and reconciliation, not a minister of profit and recognition. More on that in Safety vs Suffering.

On the other hand, many among the Wolf-spotters don't recognize their own hypocrisy when it comes to feelings of love and entitlement. I will watch their channels on YouTube, and even agree with everything they said in their rebuke against someone's teaching or behavior. However, when someone in the comment section asks a fair question, the one who made the video responds with cheeky, self-righteous, or condescending comments.

Apparently, these people think "nit-picking" is a spiritual gift. If I were to say, "I'm trying to do better in my Christian walk," they will go on the attack and say, "He's basing the Christian life on his own effort! He's preaching a works-based salvation!" Or, if I were to say, "I'm done trying and I'm just giving it over to God," they will say, "He's preaching hyper-grace doctrine!" Not only that, but if I were to quote someone else's biblically sound statement, but the person I'm quoting from has some bad doctrine elsewhere, then I'm a heretic by association.

I often wonder if these people even attend church, given how they seem to think everyone who doesn't read and interpret the Bible the exact same way they do is a heretic. The phrase, "benefit of the doubt" or "innocent until proven guilty" is far removed from their discernment making. Sadly, many of these Wolf-spotters are part of a cult, if not the very leaders of the cult. I say that, because they claim the very thing that I just said, in that, "Anyone who doesn't think exactly as I (or my pastor) do (or does) is going to hell." Furthermore, whenever you watch enough of that particular Wolf-spotter's videos, all kinds of bad teachings and attitudes start to surface.

Even if such a person has a whole list of preachers and teachers they listen to, I could easily nit-pick those preachers and teachers myself. Should I do away with the Wolf-spotter? Should I not listen to those preachers or teachers? Even if someone is a heretic regarding an essential doctrine, am I forbidden to listen to *anything* they have to say about *any* subject?

However, the Wolf-spotter might say, "The teachers I listen to, even if I don't agree with everything they say, aren't swindling people out of millions of dollars and flying private jets." Perhaps, and I myself am turned off by that kind of luxury. However, how do we fairly define "luxury"? I ask, for I'm certain that almost every single pastor makes a living as a pastor, right? Even the pastors the Wolf-spotters think to be legitimate in all likelihood earn a salary for being a pastor.

They might say, "Yes, but they only make $50,000 a year, not $500,000 a year." Perhaps, but your pastor has a congregation of 500 people, whereas the mega-church pastor has a congregation of 5,000 people. Both pastors are making $100 a year per congregant, and I'm certain that both their congregations agreed to their salary. Your pastor bought a new car that was $40,000, whereas the mega-church pastor bought a new car for $400,000. Your pastor bought a $300,000 house, whereas the mega-church pastor bought a house for $3,000,000.

Your pastor bought a boat that he doesn't need, whereas the mega-church pastor bought a plane. Your pastor took a vacation and pampered himself at tropical resort on an island somewhere, whereas the mega-church pastor did the exact same thing, only it was a nicer hotel and spa. What is the magical number in which your earning/spending ratio goes from reasonable to excessive? Let's go further, shall we?

How much is *your own* salary? How much was *your* car? How much was *your* house? How many unnecessary toys and tools do you have laying around *your* house, such as campers, ATVs, dirt bikes, pools, jet skis, guns, etc.? How much did *you* spend on *your* last vacation or restaurant tab? Just take a moment and reflect on that. Nevertheless, whether you've gained the whole world or forsook it, if you have not *love*, you have nothing. Whether you live in a mansion, or under a bridge, if you have not love, you are nothing. It is better to be rich and grateful than to be poor and self-righteous. More on that in <u>Safety vs Suffering</u>.

1 Corinthians 13: 4-7 says, "Love is patient, love is kind, it is not jealous; love does not brag, it is not arrogant. It does not act disgracefully, it does not seek its own benefit; it is not provoked, does not keep an account of a wrong suffered, it does not rejoice in unrighteousness, but rejoices with the truth; it keeps every confidence, it believes all things, hopes all things, endures all things."

Here's the list of what love *is*:

1) Patient

2) Kind

3) Rejoices in Truth

4) Keeps Every Confidence

5) Believes All Things

6) Hopes All Things

7) Endures All Things

And here's a list of what love *is not*:

1) Jealous

2) Bragging

3) Arrogant

4) Acting Disgracefully

5) Seeking Its Own Benefit

6) Easily Provoked

7) Keeping an Account of a Wrong Suffered

8) Rejoicing in Unrighteousness

Which list does your life and attitude resemble most? Sadly, those who are jealous, arrogant, and all the rest are typically unable to recognize such qualities in themselves. Even if they do recognize them, they are quick to justify their behaviors and attitudes, not repent of them.

However, to those who are quick to call Wolf-spotters unloving simply because they disagree with someone's theology or methods, think for a moment: Which list does "Rejoices in Truth" fall under? Which list does "Rejoices in Unrighteousness" fall under? If the Wolf-spotter's primary concern is speaking truth and rebuking unrighteousness, then they are not automatically being unloving, even if the Wolf-spotter is the one in doctrinal error, themselves! However, the Wolf-spotter could indeed fall under the "unloving list" for other reasons.

They could brag or be arrogant about being more educated and having a Seminary degree. To which, unless you have a degree yourself, you aren't smart enough (I mean, "spiritual" enough) to pose an argument against them. Or, they resort to name calling instead of posing an argument, which isn't very kind or patient. The Wolf-spotter might say, "Jesus called the Pharisees a brood of vipers!" Yes, but He also said that anyone who says to his brother, "You fool!" is liable to fiery hell (Matthew 5:22). So, such name calling shouldn't be tossed about lightly, especially for the sake of "winning the argument". Besides, what's the point of winning the argument if you've lost the person?

Regarding those who are amongst the Charismatic circles, think about this: If a man (or woman) claims to be anointed by God, but lacks the *patience* or *kindness* to deal with those who disagree, especially when the "anointed" are making questionable decisions that aren't *keeping every confidence,* what does that say about the anointed? On the other hand, many a false prophet hides behind a smile and kind disposition, which makes them highly likeable. So, if a likeable false prophet is being attacked by an angry (if not foul-mouthed) Wolf-spotter, how persuasive is the Wolf-spotter going to be towards those who are captivated by the false-prophet's charm?

Yes, love believes all things, but does that mean believing in anything and everything? Does that mean believing the color blue has a flavor? That 2+2=5? That all paths lead to Heaven or that Jesus isn't the Son of God? Are we to believe and teach such things simply because we don't want to be "unloving" towards those who do?

Yes, love hopes all things, but does that mean *anything* is possible? Can I place my hope in an idol of my own making and it not be a fool's hope? Can I hope in my own opinion as to how salvation works and indeed receive salvation? That my loved ones who rejected Christ and died will get a second chance after death even though there is no biblical foundation for such a teaching?

Yes, love endures all things, but does that mean to turn a blind eye to sin? If so, and God is love, why does *He* not turn a blind eye to it? Why would He bother to die for sin? Why are we to hold each other accountable regarding sin if we aren't to do anything about sin?

So, what does it mean that love believes, hopes, and endures all things? Perhaps "all things" is regarding all things pertaining to truth, given how we are to rejoice in truth. And the truth is, we are to desire righteousness, not unrighteousness. Furthermore, we must be able to differentiate between the two. Also, those who want to live righteously we be hated by the unrighteous. And lastly, if we should suffer for the sake of righteousness, we are to rejoice, for our reward in heaven is great!

Or, could it be that believing, hoping, and enduring all things is regarding the idea of "innocent until proven guilty" or "benefit of the doubt"? Meaning, we shouldn't be quick to accusation, but should thoroughly investigate a matter before pronouncing judgement. And even if the investigation should lead us into making a disappointing conclusion, should our initial reaction be excommunication, or should it be reconciliation? Even Jesus said if we see a fellow Christian in sin (or error) and they refuse to repent (or change their mind), we are only to excommunicate them after a third warning. And even then, it is to be done as a congregation, not the opinion of a single individual.

Yet, if a church tolerates such things, if not embraces such things (rejoicing in unrighteousness) then how much error should a Bible loving individual endure until they leave the church and go elsewhere? Such is a matter of the individual's conscience. Should you stay in the hope of turning the church around, or should you shake the dust off your feet and move on to the next church? Who knows?

1 Corinthians 13: 8-13 says, "Love never fails; but if there are gifts of prophecy, they *will* be done away with; if there are tongues, they *will* cease; if there is knowledge, it *will* be done away with. For we know *in part* and prophesy *in part*; but when the *perfect* comes, the partial will be done away with. When I was a child, I used to speak like a child, think like a child, reason like a child; when I became a man, I did away with childish things. For now, *we* see in a mirror dimly, but then face to face; now *I* know in part, but then *I* will know fully, just as *I* also have been fully known. But

now these three: faith, hope, and love remain; but the greatest of these is love."

This is the passage that Cessationists refer to when justifying their belief that gifts of tongues and prophecy are no longer functioning. Yes, they will cease, but when does it say they will cease? It says "When the perfect comes". Cessationists claim the "perfect" being referenced in this passage is referring to the Bible. That being, the day when all the New Testament writings were gathered into one place and made cannon.

Why do they make this assumption? Because Paul says "We know in part, we prophesy in part but when the [official and full New Testament] comes, the partial will be done away with... For now, we see through a mirror dimly, but then, face to face; now I know in part, but then I will know fully, just as I have been fully known."

The time period in which the New Testament was officially assembled and recognized is highly debated. However, out of all the websites I checked, the earliest anyone thinks the New Testament to be made cannon was in the late 2nd century or early 3rd century, 175-225 AD. However, Paul is believed to have been executed in 67 AD, 100 years before the earliest estimations of the New Testament. Even if you want to say that when Paul says "We" he means the church in general, that doesn't explain why he says "I". That being, "Now I know in part, but then I will know fully, just as I also have been fully known."

Nevertheless, John's Gospel and Revelation were certainly written after Paul's death. So, even if Paul had read everything else written before his death, he never knew the full New Testament. Even if you want to still claim that Paul was referring to the New Testament, you have other issues to contend with. If the New Testament was supposed to bring perfect clarity to all prophecy, then it fails miserably, given all the different opinions on Revelation alone. The point is, the "perfect" referred to by Paul is not the New Testament, though I believe in the inerrancy of Scripture.

So, what is the "perfect" Paul is referring to? Is he talking about:

1) Life after death, when Christians enter paradise?

2) Jesus Christ at the second coming?

3) Judgement Day, when all will be revealed, including hidden sins and motives?

4) The new heavens and new earth, when all will be made new?

I believe it to be a combination of the last 3 possibilities, given they will all happen in the same instant. Meaning, the "perfect" has yet to come, and tongues and prophecy are still functioning today in some capacity. However, Paul says something interesting in the passage. He says, "When I was a child, I used to speak like a child, think like a child, reason like a child; when I became a man, I did away with childish things." Why would he throw that statement in there as a comparison to the current state of prophecy (at the time) and what is to become of it? Is Paul saying when he was younger and immature in the faith he relied heavily on prophetic revelation, but now that he is older, he doesn't rely on it as much? Is he saying that as he matured in his faith that prophecy and tongues became less frequent in his personal life?

Given my own experiences, I can certainly see that as a possibility. As I became more solid in my faith, the frequency of dreams and visions incredibly diminished to the point where it only happens a few times a year, whereas it could be a few times a week when it started. It started when I was 21, and I'm only 30 now.

Nevertheless, my experience is subjective to those who can't say for certain whether I'm lying or not, so we will stick with Paul.

Paul is comparing his life to the church experience in this passage. Meaning, as the church itself grows and matures, the necessity of prophecy and tongues will *decrease*, not increase. Also, I'm certain that access to the entire Bible is a major step in the church's maturity and growth. To which, if a *specific* church *building* has everyone inside speaking in tongues and prophesying, it is for one of four reasons:

1) Everyone with the gift of tongues and prophecy in the global church gathered into a few single locations for the sake of not feeling like freaks, even though it's in disobedience to the purpose of Christ having a body with different parts for different functions for the sake of the rest of the body, as mentioned in 1 Corinthians 12.

2) Everyone in those few church buildings is highly immature in the faith and Biblical understanding, to which, God has to give them an extra measure of the Spirit to help speed things along.

3) There are people in those specific church buildings who are fake or so spiritually uneducated that they don't know the difference between a prophetic word, a demonic word, or pure hallucinations or dreams brought on by food or drugs, etc.

4) A combination of the three.

I read where one so-called prophet claimed that Donald Trump was going to win a 2nd term in 2020. When Trump lost, he back-pedaled and claimed that he misinterpreted the prophecy. He even gave the transcript of all the prophecies he received over the course of Trump's 1st term. I could tell they weren't real prophecies just by what was supposedly being said. Verbatim, the so-called prophet claimed that God said, "If Trump continues to act the way he does, I don't believe he will win a 2nd term." And there were plenty of similar prophecies the prophet claimed to receive.

First of all, if the motif of uncertainty was going on for *years*, how could you possibly *misinterpret* that as "Trump *will* win"? Secondly, when in the *entirety* of the Bible has God *ever* spoken in uncertain terms such as "I don't believe"? Whenever God gave a word to a prophet, the terms were *always* certain. That being, "If *this* happens, then *that* will happen. If *that* happens, then *this* will happen". If he knew his Bible the way he should, then he would know what he was hearing wasn't of God, if he indeed actually heard something and isn't purely making it up. As mentioned, if you knew your Bible, you wouldn't be so easily deceived by "prophets", for a true prophet can't receive a word from God that is contrary to the Bible.

Nevertheless, I hear Cessationists say, "If prophecy is still going on today, then we would have to keep adding to the Bible! Therefore, it can't be for today!" I understand the concern, but the concern exists because of an illogical pretense. That being, if prophecy still exists, then we would *have to* keep adding to the Bible. But there were many people in Paul's lifetime, who weren't even apostles, but had the gift of prophecy. Furthermore, hardly any of their prophecies were ever written down in Scripture. If all prophecy has to be written down, then the New Testament writers were in disobedience. In fact, not everything that Jesus said while He was *on the earth* was written down. The point being, we don't have to hold modern prophecies to be equal to Scripture.

Regardless of what you think of what I've written, one thing is certain: Faith, hope, and love remain, but the greatest of these is love. Thus, whether you think prophecy and tongues are for today or not, faith, hope, and love *are* for today. And if you lack these three things, especially love, then your own opinion on prophecy and tongues is worthless.

CHARISMATICS VS CESSATIONISTS (PART THREE)

1 Corinthians 14: 1-5: "Pursue love, yet earnestly desire spiritual gifts, but especially that you may *prophesy*. <u>For the one who speaks in a tongue does not speak to *people*, but to *God*; for *no one* understands, but in his spirit, he speaks mysteries. But the one who prophesies speaks to people for edification, exhortation, and consolation.</u> The one who speaks in a tongue edifies himself; but the one who prophesies edifies the church. Now I wish that you all spoke in tongues, but rather that you would prophesy; and greater is the one who prophesies than the one who speaks in tongues, unless he interprets, so that the church may receive edification."

In the context of the last chapter, Paul is affirming that love is the primary concern for our lives, but we are to desire other spiritual gifts. However, he is clearly stating it is better to prophesy than to have any other spiritual gift, even tongues. For tongues only benefit the person speaking, but prophecy benefits everyone. Yet, many Charismatic teachers and churches emphasize tongues to the highest degree and downplay everything else. Furthermore, hardly anyone says anything about interpreting tongues. If we are to not only look after our own interests, but are to look after the interests of others, why do we desire something, even a spiritual gift, that only benefits ourselves? That being, if our primary focus is to love others, why are we not pursuing it? Or, why are we making love a secondary issue?

1 Corinthians 14: 6-12 says, "But now, brothers and sisters, if I come to you speaking in tongues, how will I benefit you unless I speak to you either by way of *revelation*, or of *knowledge*, or of *prophecy*, or of *teaching*? Yet even lifeless instruments, whether flute or harp, in producing a sound, if they do not produce a distinction in the tones, how will it be known what is played on the flute or on the harp? For if the trumpet produces an indistinct sound, who will prepare himself for battle? So you too, unless you produce intelligible speech by the tongue, how will it be known what is spoken? For you will just be talking to the air. There are, perhaps, a great many kinds of languages in the world, and none is incapable of meaning. So, if I do not know the meaning of the language, I will be unintelligible to the one who speaks, and the one who speaks will be unintelligible to me. So, you too, since you are eager to possess spiritual gifts, strive to excel for the edification of the church."

Again, Paul is not saying we shouldn't desire to speak in tongues at all. The point he is making is that unless the tongue you are speaking is understandable, then it does not benefit the church. Inasmuch, Paul elevates revelation, knowledge, prophecy, and teaching to be superior gifts than that of speaking in tongues. Meaning, even if speaking in tongues is a prayer language between you and God, and you do indeed have the gift, do not think you are somehow more spiritual or important than those who are gifted in revelation, knowledge, teaching, and prophecy.

However, Cessationists emphasize teaching and knowledge over revelation, prophecy, and tongues. It makes sense for them to do so, given they believe revelation, prophecy, and tongues are no longer in operation. To which, if a Charismatic has a spiritual experience, but doesn't have a biblical teaching to back up the experience, the Charismatic is then immediately rebuked by the Cessationist as a fraud.

Would that have been a fair approach to the man who was born blind and healed in John 9? The man was certainly blind from birth, but because he didn't have a biblical argument to explain what happened to him, the Pharisees threw him out of the syna-gogue. Granted, the Pharisees mainly rejected the man who was healed because he praised Jesus and gave Him the credit for the healing. To which, I'm not equating Christ affirming Cessationists to Christ denying Pharisees, but it begs the question: If someone claims to have an experience and gives glory to God, is it fair to immediately condemn the person as a liar or blasphemer? Of course, not. However, that doesn't mean the one who had an experience shouldn't look for a biblical answer; a notion that Paul affirms in the next few verses.

For 1 Corinthians 14: 13-19 says, "Therefore, one who speaks in a tongue is to *pray that he may interpret*. For if I pray in a tongue, my spirit prays, but my mind is unproductive. What is the out-come then? I will pray with the spirit, but I will *pray with the mind* also; I will sing with the spirit, but I will *sing with the mind* also. For otherwise, if you bless God in the spirit only, how will the one who occupies the place of the outsider know to say the "Amen" at your giving of thanks, since he does not understand what you are saying? For *you are* giving thanks well enough, but the other person *is not edified*. I thank God, I speak in tongues more than you all; nevertheless, *in church* I prefer to speak five words with my mind so that I may instruct others also, rather than ten thou-sand words in a tongue."

Paul again affirms that we should desire to edify others with our gifts, not just ourselves. We should desire to give clear instruction to others, not confusing attention for ourselves. We should want others to say "Amen" not "Wow". And guess what? We can look for a "Wow" even while giving a biblical teaching! For even if we teach sound doctrine, we can do so for the sake of impressing others with our knowledge instead of for their edification. For even Paul says there are those who preach Christ out of selfish ambition. Thus, be wary of your attitude.

1 Corinthians 14: 20-25 says, "Brothers and sisters, do not be *children* in your thinking; yet in evil be infants, but in your thinking be *mature*. In the Law it is written: 'By MEN OF STRANGE TONGUES AND BY THE LIPS OF STRANGERS I WILL SPEAK TO THIS PEOPLE, AND EVEN SO THEY WILL NOT LISTEN TO ME,' says the Lord. So then, tongues are for a sign, not to those who believe but to unbelievers; but prophecy is not for unbelievers, but for those who believe. Therefore, if the whole church gathers together and *all* the people speak in tongues, and outsiders or unbelievers enter, will they not say that you are *insane*? But if all prophesy, and an unbeliever or an outsider enters, he is convicted by all, he is called to account by all; the secrets of his heart are disclosed; and so, he will fall on his face and worship God, declaring that God is certainly among you."

Paul says speaking in tongues is a sign for *unbelievers*, not believers. Yet, he also says if everyone in your church speaks in tongues, unbelievers who enter the church will think you're insane and want to leave. What's the deal? I think what Paul is getting at is this: Speaking in tongues will *get* an unbeliever's attention, but prophecy will *keep* their attention. A woman's beauty will *get* a man's attention, but her character is what will *keep* it. If a woman is all show and no substance, a sensible man will be put off. If a church is all tongues and no prophecy or teaching, an unbeliever will see no point in staying.

However, if clear prophecy, teaching, knowledge, and revelation are being given, then the clear instruction of the Lord is being given. And if the clear instruction of the Lord is being given, then the Lord's instructions towards unbelievers are being given. And if clear instructions towards unbelievers are being given, then they will be convicted of their sin and repent. Of course, this isn't true every single time, for there are plenty who reject the clear instruction of the Lord. However, if anyone is going to repent, it will be owing to clear instruction and the moving of the Spirit.

1 Corinthians 14: 26-36 says, "What is the outcome then, brothers and sisters? When you assemble, each one has a psalm, has a teaching, has a revelation, has a tongue, has an interpretation. All things are to be done for edification. If anyone speaks in a tongue, it must be by two or at the most three, and each one in turn, and one is to interpret; but if there is no interpreter, he is to keep silent in church; and have him speak to himself and to God. Have two or three prophets speak, and have the others pass judgment. But if a revelation is made to another who is seated, then the first one is to keep silent. For you can all prophesy one by one, so that all may learn and all may be exhorted; and the spirits of prophets are subject to prophets; for God is not a God of confusion, but of peace. As in all the churches of the saints, the women are to keep silent in the churches; for they are not permitted to speak, but are to subject themselves, just as the Law also says. If they desire to learn anything, let them ask their own husbands at home; for it is improper for a woman to speak in church. Or was it from you that the word of God first went out? Or has it come to you only?"

Paul says that no more than two or three people should speak in a tongue at a time, and there is to be at least one to interpret. If there is no one to interpret, no one should speak in a tongue, but should keep it to themselves. Paul said earlier that if you speak in a tongue you should pray for an interpretation. Meaning, the one necessary interpreter can be one of the two or three that are speaking. But if you don't receive an interpretation, then you are to keep it to yourself. That is not saying you should muster the strength to suppress and silence the tongue completely, but that you shouldn't interrupt a church service for the sake of them hearing what you are saying.

However, I find it interesting that the Spirit can stir you to speak in a tongue even though there is no one around to interpret what you are saying. Meaning, there is truth that speaking in tongues can be a personal prayer language that you keep to yourself, and that an interpreter doesn't have to always be around for someone to be able to start speaking in tongues. Many Cessationists claim that someone can't even have the *ability* to speak in a tongue unless someone is present to interpret what is being said. Thus, if you start speaking in a tongue and no one can understand you, Cessationists claim you are purposefully speaking gibberish or are being influenced by demons. Yet, this passage shows such a claim to not be true. That is not to say that no one ever speaks gibberish or becomes influenced by demons, but it shouldn't be automatically assumed, either.

Furthermore, Paul says that even prophecy is to be done in an orderly manner. Only two or three people should be prophesying at a time. One gives the prophecy while the one or two other prophets sit and listen, and the prophets who are sitting weigh the prophecy and consider if it is legitimate. Meaning, even a legitimate prophet can feel as though the Lord is telling him something and be wrong! Or else, why do we need one or two other prophets to judge what he is saying?

For not all prophecy is "telling the future". Or else, how can the other two prophets determine whether or not a prophecy is legitimate until the prophecy does or doesn't happen? And if we can't know whether or not a prophecy is legitimate until it does or doesn't happen, why bother with the other two prophets to begin with? For even *unbelievers* will be able to make that judgement when it does or doesn't happen.

However, there are prophecies of the future that can be refuted at the moment of being heard. As mentioned in the last chapter, I could tell the so-called prophet wasn't speaking for God about the reelection of Donald Trump just by him saying that God said, "*I don't believe* he will win". I would have known it was false long before the election took place. (And whether or not the election was rigged is irrelevant to Trump's behavior beforehand. More on that in Culture vs Counter-Culture.)

Furthermore, I heard a woman twist the phrase "you can all prophesy" to mean "everyone in the church has the ability to prophesy". However, that would go against what Paul said earlier about how not everyone has the gift of prophecy. In the context of the statement, Paul is referring to the group of two or three, not the whole congregation. Ironically, she doesn't read a few verses further about women not being allowed to speak in church.

Inasmuch, I do find it strange that Paul uses this as an opportunity to say, "Women are to remain silent in church". I had many unpleasant discussions during online dating on this subject. Even women who labeled themselves as "Very Conservative" were incredibly liberal, if not hostile, on this subject. I was considering devoting an entire chapter on the role of women in church, but I spoke a great deal on that in *No Filter*. However, I wasn't having these particular conversations until after I already published it. Also, there is enough room in this chapter to discuss the main themes of those conversations.

The same woman who was trying to convince me that "The letter kills, but the Spirit gives life", was also saying the instruction for women not to speak in church was only for the church in Corinth. However, the passage clearly states "As in *all the churches* of the saints, the women are to remain silent in the *churches*." It was this conversation, as well as others, that prompted me to write this book. For even though I had biblical answers to their questions, I didn't always have the *best* biblical answers.

If the instructions for speaking in tongues is of any benefit, I don't think women were to be *completely* silent. For a person speaking in a tongue without an interpreter can continue to speak in a tongue if they aren't being disruptive to the rest of the church. Even though the one speaking in a tongue is to remain silent, that doesn't mean *completely* silent. Also, the instruction is "If they desire to learn anything, let them ask their own husbands at home".

This isn't a prohibition of women from speaking in tongues, or even prophesying, but a prohibition to disrupt the church service by asking questions. However, I don't think quietly and quickly leaning over to your husband asking, "What does that word mean?" is prohibited, but shouting, "Excuse me, pastor, but what does that word mean?!" However, is it necessarily considered polite for even a man to interrupt like that, or to have a continuing conversation with his buddy that's distracting to those near them? Also, the passage says, "If they desire to learn anything", which is another reason why I don't think women are prohibited from speaking in a tongue or prophesying.

For Paul says in 2 Timothy 2: 11-12 "A woman must quietly receive instruction with entire submissiveness. But I do not allow a woman to <u>teach or to exercise authority</u> over a man, but to remain quiet." To which, Paul has already made it clear that tongues and prophecy are distinct from teaching and eldership.

Also, Acts 21: 8-9 says, "On the next day we left and came to Caesarea, and entering the house of Philip the evangelist, who was one of the seven, we stayed with him. Now this man had four virgin daughters who were prophetesses." When Luke writes that Philip was one of the seven, he is referring to the seven men who

60

were chosen to serve the widows in the church in Acts 6:5. If his four daughters were prophetesses within a church, were they only to prophesy at home? I don't think so.

However, Acts 21: 10-11 continues and says, "As we were staying there for some days, <u>a prophet named Agabus came down from Judea</u>. And coming to us, *he* took Paul's belt and bound *his* own feet and hands, and said, "This is what the Holy Spirit says: 'In this way the Jews at Jerusalem will bind the man who owns this belt and deliver him into the hands of the Gentiles.'"

If Paul is staying in a house with four prophetesses, why would God send another prophet from Judea to relay a prophecy to Paul regarding his future? Was it because Agabus was a man? Was it because the women were forbidden to speak even within their own home? To which, what is the point of them being prophetesses to begin with if they can't even speak in their own home? Unless they are only allowed to prophesy amongst other women and children, I'm certain something else is going on. That being, not all prophecy is "telling the future". Also, God simply works in mysterious ways which aren't specifically explained in this passage.

Also, regarding the prohibition against a woman teaching and exercising authority over a man, I have this <u>opinion</u>: There are *circumstances* in which a woman is able to teach or exercise authority over a man, and the prohibition is a general rule. What's my biblical basis? I'm glad you asked. In Judges 4, we have the story of Deborah and Barak. I won't go into the whole story, but give a brief summary of the situation.

Judges 4: 1-10: <u>Then the *sons* of Israel again did evil in the sight of the LORD, after Ehud died</u>. So the LORD sold them into the hand of Jabin king of Canaan, who reigned in Hazor; and the commander of his army was Sisera, who lived in Harosheth-hagoyim.

The *sons* of Israel cried out to the LORD; for he had nine hundred iron chariots, and he oppressed the *sons* of Israel severely for twenty years.

Now Deborah, a *prophetess*, the wife of Lappidoth, was *judging* Israel at that time. She used to sit under the palm tree of Deborah between Ramah and Bethel in the hill country of Ephraim; and the *sons* of Israel went up to her for judgment. Now she sent word and summoned Barak the son of Abinoam from Kedesh-naphtali, and said to him, "The LORD, the God of Israel, *has indeed* commanded, 'Go and march to Mount Tabor, and take with you ten thousand men from the sons of Naphtali and from the sons of Zebulun. I will draw out to you Sisera, the commander of Jabin's army, with his chariots and his many troops to the river Kishon, and I will hand him over to you.'" Then Barak said to her, "If *you* will go with me, *then* I will go; but if you will not go with me, I will not go." She said, "I will certainly go with you; however, the fame shall not be yours on the journey that you are about to take, for the LORD will sell Sisera into the hand of a woman." Then Deborah got up and went with Barak to Kedesh. Barak summoned Zebulun and Naphtali to Kedesh, and ten thousand men went up with him; Deborah also went up with him. (NASB)

In the context of the story, Israel has forsaken the Lord and has been oppressed by a foreign king for twenty years. During this time, Deborah is not only a prophetess, but a judge over Israel. Not a judge in the manner of Ehud, Samson, or Gideon, who were civilians hand-picked by God to exact vengeance on the enemies of Israel, but a judge in the manner of Moses. That being, she exercised authority over men by pronouncing judgements in civil and judicial matters.

However, given the context of Judges, she wasn't a judge simply because it was perfectly fine for a woman to be a judge in any and all circumstances. She was a judge because the men of Israel were pathetic and evil. Even Barak, the civilian who is the best man for the job of rescuing Israel, has to have his arm twisted by Deborah to get him to do it. Furthermore, the phrase "the God of Israel has indeed commanded", gives the impression that Barak has already been told what to do, and yet, he has to be told multiple times.

Even if Deborah is the first to tell him, his reluctancy is still telling of his character, given he says, "I won't go unless you go with me." He won't go simply because it's the command of the Lord, but because a righteous woman will go with him. She agrees to go with him, but lets him know he won't get the credit, but *she* will. She is doing everything she can to tell Barak to "man up" and do the will of God, and he still only does so reluctantly.

If Israel was doing what it should have been doing from the beginning, there would have been no need of Deborah. But because there wasn't a single man in all of Israel who was willing to do the work of the Lord, God chose Deborah to fill the role. Thus, there are circumstances in which a woman can teach or exercise authority over a man, although those circumstances are extreme.

Even Jesus said in Matthew 12 that, although it was unlawful for David and his companions to eat the showbread, for it was only allowed to be eaten by the priests, they did not sin in eating it because the need was great and the circumstances were extreme. To which, Jesus said, "If you knew what God meant when He said, 'I require mercy, not sacrifice,' you wouldn't condemn the innocent." To which, I would think, if there is a need for a teaching or authoritative position in which there are no men who are able or willing to fill the position, then a woman is allowed to fill the position.

However, just as someone speaking in a tongue should pray for an interpretation, a woman should first pray that God would raise up a man for the position. And if she takes the position, it should be for the sake of edifying and exhorting the men so that one day a man will be able to take her place. And if that offends women, remember this: Even a man in such a position should edify and exhort his church to the point that another man will eventually take his place.

Nevertheless, if I walk into a church and see a woman preaching behind the pulpit, I know immediately that something is wrong with the church. For if a woman is behind the pulpit, it is for one of four reasons:

1) The church is unrestrained due to "special revelations" that supposedly overrule the authority of scripture, as we have already discussed.

2) The church is theologically/politically liberal and doesn't really care about the authority of scripture because they are more concerned about being culturally acceptable, which we will talk about later in Culture vs Counter-Culture.

3) The church is of a certain denomination or congregation who has never read that a woman shouldn't teach or exercise authority over a man, or is under the impression that the Greek actually says that a wife shouldn't teach or exercise authority over her husband. To which, what else have they left out or misinterpreted?

4) The church is so weak and immature that a God-fearing woman has to rise up and do the job of a man, in which I would be moved to pray and see if God wants me to fill the position, myself.

However, regardless of how you feel about what your pastor says, what culture says, or what I have said, one thing is clear: 1 Corinthians 14: 37-38 says, "If *anyone* [in the present or in the future] thinks that he is a prophet or spiritual, <u>let him recognize that the things which I write to you are the *Lord's* commandment.</u> But if *anyone* [in the present or in the future] does not recognize this, *he* <u>is not recognized</u>."

If I am incorrect in anything I have written regarding my interpretations of Paul's instructions, then ignore the interpretation and keep to the actual instruction. However, if I have interpreted Paul correctly, then obey what I have written. For if you don't, it isn't I who you are rebelling against, but Paul. And if you don't listen to Paul, then it isn't Paul you are rebelling against, but God.

As mentioned, Jesus affirmed Peter, and Peter affirmed Paul. If we are not to trust Peter regarding what he said of Paul and what he says, then why should we trust Peter regarding Jesus and what *He* says? If you want to say the New Testament has been tampered with in one area, why should we think the tricksters didn't tamper with other areas, if not the whole Bible?

In closing, 1 Corinthians 14: 39-40 says, "Therefore, my brothers and sisters, earnestly desire to prophesy, and do not forbid speaking in tongues. But *all things* <u>must be done properly and in an orderly way</u>."

SAFETY VS SUFFERING

One of the reasons I have a hard time listening to most mainstream preachers and teachers isn't necessarily their income or investments, but their incompetence. That being, they're incapable of having a consistent argument, whether it be on the Bible or their personal opinions. For there are plenty of preachers and teachers who live modest lifestyles, yet, preach and teach things that are completely nonsensical. And one of the main teachings that is common in America, and mainly any "free" country, is this: Jesus died so you can be safe and secure, not suffer and struggle.

A pastor I listen to once said, "Any cult is of Satan, and Satan always attacks two things: Scripture and the cross." I have already dealt a great deal with those who attack Scripture, so let us go into the cross. For although it isn't as universal as Scripture and the cross, there are two other things that mark almost every cult: False teachings on persecution and false teachings about marriage and sex.

Why would I want to go into those two subjects when dealing with the cross? Because those who preach and teach that the cross brought safety and security typically pervert the teachings on persecution and sexual purity, as well. For they teach the Christian's happiness is paramount to the Christian life, no matter where the Christian hopes to find that happiness.

One man I have watched on television was a "marriage expert" who had been counseling on marriage for over 40 years. Meaning, this man's specialty was marriage and what the Bible says about it. Meaning, he should know what Jesus said about marriage and divorce in Matthew 5:32, or what Paul says about marriage and divorce in 1 Corinthians 7. However, when a woman asked him whether or not she could remarry after getting her *third* divorce, without any hesitation or further inquiry, he said, "Absolutely! God wants us to be happy."

This man was instrumental in helping me to learn what it meant for a man to love his wife as Christ loved the church, yet, he would have such an opinion as *that*? Does he truly understand the cross to begin with? Or does he value the cross but not Scripture? Thus, before I go into the false-teachings of the cross, I shall define what the cross truly is.

As I mentioned in *No Filter*, the definition of sin is to be unloving. For if righteousness is defined as loving God with all your heart, soul, mind, and strength, and to love your neighbor as yourself, then unrighteousness is to have not loved God or others. When Adam and Eve sinned, however minor it may seem, eating the fruit of the tree was being unloving towards God. But why can't God simply overlook it? Because overlooking sin would not be an act of love, but apathy. Besides, you are not offending a single individual when sinning against God, but three: Father, Son, and Holy Spirit.

The confusion of the doctrine of the Trinity boils down to this: How can God be one person and three persons at the same time? That being, how can a single individual be three individuals at the same time? The confusion is brought about because we have been trained to think the word "God" has a single definition. That being, we think God can only mean "single individual". However, a word can have multiple definitions. Inasmuch, the biblical definition of "God" is within the realm of "The community of three eternal individuals who have forever co-existed in perfect harmony and hierarchy, despite each being equally capable and competent as the others, and are the ultimate source of all existence, purpose, and destiny".

The concept of eternity is hard to grasp, but it's a necessary requirement for existence. For if nothing is eternal, how is it we exist? If there was absolutely nothing, a complete vacuum of existence, how did existence come about? Thus, the ultimate source of existence has to be eternal. Furthermore, it must be self-sufficient and stable. That being, it doesn't need a source outside of itself to sustain it, nor can it ever change. It cannot increase or decrease. All such definitions and qualities are attributes of God which can be found in Scripture.

However, God isn't an impersonal force of nature, but a supernatural community of individuals. That being, They are beings with emotions and feelings. If They are going to get along and accomplish anything, They not only have to be organized in a hierarchical structure of authority (Father, Son, Holy Spirit) but They have to love each other to keep that order. For if the Father didn't love the Son or Holy Spirit, He would become a tyrant. If the Son and Holy Spirit didn't love the Father, they would want to rebel against Him. To which, love is what keeps Them in hierarchy and harmony, and that love is perfect and unshakeable. And even though each member of the Trinity is just as capable and competent as the rest, having all the same attributes, they willingly choose to follow the hierarchy out of that love.

Thus, whenever we sin, even if directly against a single member of the Trinity, all three members are offended in some capacity. How can one member of the Celestial Community say He perfectly and unshakably loves the other members of the Community, and yet, overlooks and casually dismisses an act of hatred against Them?

How can He love the other members of the Community and not be angered when someone hatefully offends Them? How could He simply forgive the sinner unless the other members are also willing to forgive the sinner? Fortunately, our God is such a God!

To which, you may still ask, "How is it fair that one sin is punishable by eternal fiery torment? What kind of loving God could do such a thing?" To which, I say, "If God is a perfectly loving God, how can He *not* punish sin in such a way?" Let me explain:

God is so loving, He finds even a single act of hatred to be so reprehensible and contemptable, that the only just action for such a loving God to take is to kill that hateful person and have that sinner suffer the worst fate imaginable. But God is also so loving, that even though we were His enemies by sinning and committing *multiple* acts of hatred every day of our lives, He not only didn't kill us where we stood, but lovingly sent His own Son to take our place on the cross, and the Son willingly gave His life out of love for us and the Father's will. Inasmuch, anyone who repents of their hatred and pursues to fully love God and others will not only be saved from that eternal fiery fate, but will be adopted as the sons and daughters of God; being a co-heir with Christ and receiving the exact same measure of harmonious love from the Father that the Father has for the Son. That's how loving God is! Who would hate such a God?!

Unfortunately, as I pointed out in *No Filter*, most people *do* hate that God. Even *I* once hated that God. Why? For I was under the impression that Jesus died to make me *physically* safe and secure, not *spiritually* safe and secure. I thought the Christian life was supposed to be happy and peaceful, but my childhood wasn't happy and peaceful. Sure, there were plenty of people out there with worse childhoods and current living situations than I had, but an angry and self-centered middle-schooler doesn't think in such extrospective measures.

If God was completely sovereign over every aspect of existence, then nothing unpleasant could happen to me unless He made it happen. To which, in my mind, if being a Christian meant having a safe and secure life, and yet, God was allowing, if not directly causing my life to be miserable, then He must hate me. Meaning, God couldn't be trusted, nor was He good, as far as I was concerned.

However, Hebrews 11:1 says, "Now faith is the *certainty* of things hoped for, a *proof* of things not seen." Furthermore, verse 6 says, "And without faith it is impossible to please Him, for the one who comes to God must believe that He exists, and that <u>He proves to be One who rewards those who seek Him.</u>" We are to live by faith, not by sight. We are to conform our lives to the promises of God's word, not the pressures of this life.

For Romans 8:28 says, "And we know that <u>God causes *all* things to work together for good to those who love God,</u> to those who are called according to His purpose." And verses 35-39 say, '<u>Who will separate us from the love of Christ? Will tribulation, or trouble, or persecution, or famine, or nakedness, or danger, or sword</u>? Just as it is written: "FOR YOUR SAKE WE ARE KILLED ALL DAY LONG; WE WERE REGARDED AS SHEEP TO BE SLAUGHTERED.' But <u>in *all* these things we overwhelmingly conquer through Him who loved us.</u> For I am convinced that neither death, nor life, nor angels, nor principalities, nor things present, nor things to come, nor powers, nor height, nor depth, nor any other created thing will be able to separate us from the love of God that is in Christ Jesus our Lord."

How do these texts measure up to the false-teachings of safety and security? Jesus never promised us that storms wouldn't come, but that we would withstand the storm. For He said in Matthew 7: 24-27 "Therefore, *everyone* who hears these words of Mine, *and acts on them*, will be like a wise man who built his house on the rock. And <u>the rain fell and the floods came, and the winds blew</u>

and slammed against that house; *and yet it did not fall,* for it had been founded on the rock. And everyone who hears these words of Mine, and *does not* act on them, will be like a foolish man who built his house on the sand. And the rain fell and the floods came, and the winds blew and slammed against that house; and it fell— and its collapse was great."

And what do the words of Christ say? 2 Timothy 3: 10-17 says, "Now you followed my teaching, conduct, purpose, faith, patience, love, perseverance, persecutions, and sufferings, such as hap-pened to me at Antioch, at Iconium and at Lystra; what persecu-tions I endured, and out of them all the Lord rescued me! Indeed, *all* who desire to live godly in Christ Jesus *will be* persecuted. But evil men and impostors will proceed from bad to worse, deceiving and being deceived. You, however, continue in the things you have learned and become convinced of, knowing from whom you have learned them, and that from childhood you have known the *sacred writings* which are able to give you the wisdom that leads to salvation through faith which is in Christ Jesus. *All* Scripture is inspired by God and profitable for teaching, for reproof, for cor-rection, for training in righteousness; so that the man of God may be adequate, equipped for every good work."

Furthermore, 2 Corinthians 4: 7-12 says, "But we have this trea-sure [the Gospel] in earthen containers, so that the extraordinary greatness of the power will be of God and not from ourselves; we are *afflicted* in every way, but not crushed; *perplexed*, but not despairing; *persecuted*, but not abandoned; *struck down*, but not destroyed; always carrying around in the body the dying of Jesus, so that the life of Jesus may also be revealed in our body. For we who live are constantly being handed over to death because of Jesus, so that the life of Jesus may also be revealed in our mortal flesh. So, death works in us, but life in you."

I will get into "earthen containers" in <u>Jars of Clay</u>. But first, what is the Gospel? It is what I mentioned earlier about God being so loving so as to send His Son to die to save sinners, even though we were His enemies. Yet, as mentioned, most people hate that God. To which, they will hate those who preach Him. For Jesus said in John 15: 18-21, "<u>If the world hates you, you know that it has hated Me before it hated you</u>. If you were of the world, the world would love you as its own; but because you are not of the world, but I chose you out of the world, because of this the world hates you. Remember the word that I said to you, '<u>A slave is not greater than his master.</u>' If they persecuted *Me*, they will perse-cute *you* as well; if they followed My word, they will follow yours also</u>. But all these things they will do to you on account of My name, because they do not know the One who sent Me."

As mentioned, false apostles never pave the way for the Gospel, but drive their cars down the roads the true apostles paved with their own blood. You only find such preachers and teachers in countries where there is safety and security for Christians. Most of these preachers and teachers say you shouldn't have to suffer at all for being a Christian, for you are a child of God and you have certain rights. Again, such men boast about their Kingdom rights, not their Gospel requirements.

Many cult leaders felt they shouldn't have to suffer for their teachings, either:

1) <u>Joseph Smith, Founder of Mormonism:</u> Gets arrested and fears for his life, to which a gun is snuck into his prison cell. A mob of men make their way to the prison, to which Joseph Smith and companions have a shoot out with the mob, with all the Mormons inside the prison being killed, including Joseph Smith.

2) <u>Jim Jones, Founder of The People's Temple:</u> Creates Jonestown and threatens any of his followers who want to leave with violence. A United States Congressman and a few other people visit Jonestown and supposedly convince Jones to let anyone go who wants to leave. However, at the airport, some of Jones' men shoot and kill the Congressman and his companions. Knowing the US government will retaliate, Jones tells his followers to drink poison or else be shot. However, Jones shoots himself in the head.

3) <u>David Koresh, Founder of the Branch Davidians:</u> Claimed to be the second-coming of Christ. He and his followers are trapped inside their building in a stand-off with police. Koresh's followers and the police have a shootout that lasts for 51 days. Police set the building on fire and everyone inside dies. Some deaths are from the fire, some from police, some from suicide, and some from fellow members. It is unsure whether Koresh shot himself or was shot by his friend.

I'm not saying that everyone who preaches safety and security is capable of such actions, but no one who take such actions, or would command such actions, is preaching the Gospel. Now, we shouldn't look for ways to *intentionally* suffer for Christ, but we shouldn't resort to violence to protect ourselves from suffering for Christ, either. If we are to be Christlike, we are to suffer as He suffered, in that we do not revile evil for evil.

On the other hand, we also shouldn't equate every suffering we face while preaching Christ as persecution. That being, just because someone gets upset at you while you're preaching the Gospel doesn't mean they hate you for Christ's sake. That being, they could be genuinely upset at your timing. They could be running late and don't care what *anyone* has to say, much less someone saying, "Repent! Before it's too late!" They could be dealing with an emergency and don't have time to deal with "There is a greater emergency! Your soul is at stake!"

Furthermore, there is a difference between being persecuted and "poking the bear". That being, there is a difference between fighting for the faith and looking for a fight in the name of faith. There is a difference between evangelism and being edgy. Paul said as long as it depends on us, we are to be at peace with all men. We are to preach the Gospel in the hope of *building* bridges, not burning them.

However, that is not to say the sole purpose of the Gospel is to build bridges with anyone and everyone. That being, if our goal as Christians is to simply get along with everyone, then the best way of getting along with everyone is to not preach the Gospel, at all! However, if the world is going to hate us for preaching the Gospel, how can the Gospel make us get along with the world? The Gospel is hostile to the world, for we preach that God calls men everywhere to repent of their sins and God-hating ways.

This is where the second part of occultism comes into focus. That being, false teachings on marriage and sex. Why is it relevant? As mentioned, false teachers focus on two things: Protection from pain and the pursuit of pleasure. Why do they teach such things? Because such things are the primary concern of sinners. That being, how can I escape worldly pain and acquire worldly pleasure?

That was the very problem in the Garden of Eden. Eve was scared she would physically die if she ate of the tree, but Satan convinced her that not only would she not physically die, but would become like God, knowing good and evil. And when she saw that it was good to eat and to make one wise, she ate of it, and gave some to her husband who was with her. As mentioned in *No Filter*, Eve was deceived by the lie, but Adam ate because *she* ate.

Even if we are convinced there is pleasure to be had, if we are convinced the pain that coincides with that pleasure is too great, then we will forsake the pleasure. Satan had to not only convince Eve that the fruit would bring pleasure, but that it wouldn't bring pain. As for Adam, he didn't want to cause an argument, for he wanted to get along with his wife and enjoy each other's company. To which, the pleasure of her company was worth more to him than the pain of argument. The desire to escape from pain and the desire to pursue pleasure is at the root of all sin.

1 John 2: 15-17 says, "Do not love the world nor the things in the world. If anyone loves the world, the love of the Father is not in him. For all that is in the world, the lust of the flesh and the lust of the eyes and the boastful pride of life, is not from the Father, but is from the world. The world is passing away and also its lusts; but the one who does the will of God continues to live forever."

Inasmuch, the greatest pleasure to be had in most people's mind is to be found in sex. However, sex was ordained by God to only be experienced between a marriage between a man and a woman. In the Garden, all the fruits were permitted, except for one. On the other hand, with sex, all the fruits are *forbidden,* except for one. If one restriction towards *food* was deemed too restrictive when our natural inclination was to love God, how much more so the restrictions towards *sex* when our natural inclination is to hate God?

Once sin entered the world, so did Murphy's Law, which states, "Anything that *can* go wrong *will* go wrong". In this case, anything that *can* be rebelled against *will* be rebelled against. Anything that *can* be disagreed upon *will* be disagreed upon. If God put the limitation *here*, we will say, "Why not *there*?" If He was to put it *there*, we would say, "Why not even *further*?" At which point, why bother to put a limitation *anywhere*?

Yes, we should only have sex with our wives, but who's to say how many wives we can have? Yes, we should only have sex with women, but who's to say we have to get married? Yes, we should only have sex with humans, but who's to say we should only have sex with women? Yes, we should only have sex with men and women, but who's to say we need their consent? Etc.

You see, the other common thread between Joseph Smith, Jim Jones, David Koresh, and other cult leaders, is their teachings and behaviors when it came to sex and marriage. Joseph Smith brought back polygamy, having 40 or so wives himself, and taught that marriage and sex continued after death, even though Jesus denies such a teaching in Matthew 22:30. Jim Jones would have frequent sex with his followers, even on stage. Not only that, but he would have sex with other men to prove how gay *they* were, meanwhile claiming that he himself was the only true heterosexual. David Koresh had forbidden the men in his congregation from having sex with their wives, claiming that only *he* was allowed to have sex with them. He also had sexual relations with underaged girls.

False teachings about sex and marriage are an attack on the cross, and any attack on the cross is of Satan. For all sexual sin is against the cross, whether it be adultery, sex before marriage, pornography, homosexuality, bestiality, etc. Why? Because sex is to be experienced within the context of a marriage between one man and one woman, and marriage is to be a symbol of the relationship that Christ has with His church.

Ephesians 5: 22-33 says, "Wives, subject yourselves to your own husbands, *as to the Lord.* For the husband is the head of the wife, as Christ also is the head of the church, He Himself being the

Savior of the body. But as the church is subject to Christ, so also the wives ought to be to their husbands in everything.

Husbands, love your wives, *just as Christ also loved the church and gave Himself up for her*, so that He might sanctify her, having cleansed her by the washing of water with the word, that He might present to Himself the church in all her glory, having no spot or wrinkle or any such thing; but that she would be holy and blameless. So husbands also ought to love their own wives as their own bodies. He who loves his own wife loves himself; for no one ever hated his own flesh, but nourishes and cherishes it, just as Christ also does the church, because we are parts of His body. FOR THIS REASON A MAN SHALL LEAVE HIS FATHER AND HIS MOTHER AND BE JOINED TO HIS WIFE, AND THE TWO SHALL BECOME ONE FLESH. This mystery is great; but I am speaking with reference to Christ and the church. Nevertheless, as for you individually, each husband is to love his own wife the same as himself, and the wife must see to it that she respects her husband."

Just like the Trinity, if a marriage is going to function to its greatest capacity, there has to be hierarchy and harmony. Furthermore, just like the Trinity, if the hierarchy and harmony is going to function to its greatest capacity, the husband and wife must respect and love each other.

However, if the husband is supposed to represent Christ and the wife represents the church, how does so-called same-sex marriage fit into the metaphor? Does Christ forsake the church and keep to Himself? Does the church come together without Christ? Two heads without bodies are dead, and two bodies without heads are dead. Christ without a church is the Messiah of no one, and a church without God is either idolatrous or atheistic. If two men get married, who is the head of who? If two women marry, who is to submit to who? Same-sex marriage is an attack on the cross, and any attack on the cross is of Satan.

But what about divorce and remarriage? Is *that* an attack on the cross, as well? Yes, if taken lightly. I shall explain. Jesus said in Matthew 5: 31-32, "Now it was said, 'WHOEVER SENDS HIS WIFE AWAY IS TO GIVE HER A CERTIFICATE OF DIVORCE'; but I say to you that <u>*everyone* who divorces his wife, except for the reason of sexual immorality, makes *her* commit adultery; and *whoever* marries a divorced woman commits adultery</u>."

Matthew 19: 3-9 goes into it further, saying, "Some Pharisees came to Jesus, testing Him and asking, 'Is it *lawful* for a man to divorce his wife for any reason at all?' And He answered and said, 'Have you not read that He who created them from the beginning MADE THEM MALE AND FEMALE, and said, 'FOR THIS REASON A MAN SHALL LEAVE HIS FATHER AND HIS MOTHER AND BE JOINED TO HIS WIFE, AND THE TWO SHALL BECOME ONE FLESH'? So, they are no longer two, but one flesh. Therefore, <u>what God has joined together, no person is to separate.</u>' They said to Him, 'Why, then, did Moses command to GIVE HER A CERTIFICATE OF DIVORCE AND SEND HER AWAY?' He said to them, '<u>Because of your hardness of heart *Moses* permitted you to divorce your wives; but *from the beginning* it has not been this way.</u> And I say to you, <u>*whoever* divorces his wife, except for sexual immorality, and marries another woman commits adultery.</u>'"

There is a lot to unpack here. Firstly, what is the commandment of Moses? Deuteronomy 24: 1-4 says, "When a man takes a wife and marries her, and it happens, *if* she finds no favor in his eyes because he has found some indecency in her, that he writes her a certificate of divorce, puts it in her hand, and sends her away from his house, and she leaves his house and goes and becomes another man's wife, and *the latter husband* turns against her, writes her a certificate of divorce and puts it in her hand, and sends her away from his house, or *if the latter husband* who took her to be his wife *dies*, then her *former husband* who sent her away is not allowed to take her *again* to be his wife, after she has been defiled; <u>for that is an *abomination* before the LORD</u>, and you shall not bring sin on the land which the LORD your God is giving you as an inheritance."

Abomination, the word that same-sex activists hate, is the same word describing what is going on here. That being, if a man divorces his wife and she becomes married to another man, and the other man divorces her or even dies, the first husband can't remarry her. Moses wasn't saying that divorcing your wife was perfectly acceptable if you give her a certificate of divorce, or that a divorced woman is perfectly free to remarry, but that *if* she got remarried, she could *never* remarry her former husband under *any* circumstance. (Furthermore, I think it's a great insight for Moses to protect women from being accused of adultery and being stoned to death by commanding a husband to have the curtesy of giving her a document proving she was no longer married to him.)

That is why Jesus said that except for sexual immorality, any man who divorces his wife and marries another commits adultery, forces her to commit adultery, and any man who marries her commits adultery. For in those times, a woman needed to be married to provide for herself. To which, if her provider is no longer providing, then she is forced to find another provider out of necessity. That being, she is forced to commit adultery for the sake of being provided for. However, any man who would marry her commits adultery in doing so.

However, don't throw the book across the room just yet, for there is more to unpack. When Jesus says "except for sexual immorality" the word for sexual immorality in the Greek is "porneias" which means "fornication; sexual sin". Yet, when Jesus says "commits adultery" the word for adultery is "moicheuthēnai" which means "adultery; sin against marriage". Why would Jesus use the word "fornication" when talking about married people? Fornication is something people who aren't married perform, right?

Porneia is a word that encompasses *all* sexual sin, whereas Moichatai is specified to marriage. Meaning, if a spouse is caught up in unrepentant sexual sin of any kind, whether it be an affair, multiple affairs, pornography, or any other sexual practice that causes an unreconcilable rift in the marriage, it is *lawful* to divorce and remarry. (Or, quite possibly, you could divorce your wife if you married her under the pretense that she was a virgin and you found out afterwards that she wasn't a virgin. Meaning, she committed fornication before the marriage. Given that Deuteronomy 22: 20-21 says such a woman is to be stoned, yet Jesus has mercy on the woman caught in adultery in John 8:11, Jesus could be saying that you can show mercy towards your wife by divorcing her instead of stoning her. Joseph was considered a righteous man when he sought to divorce Mary in Matthew 1:19. For even though Joseph and Mary were only betrothed at the time, betrothals were legally binding and not a simple formality like modern engagements. However, given that the law to stone women who lied about being a virgin was only for Israelites, it wouldn't make much since in the context of "anyone and everyone".)

Why is unrepentant sexual sin a justifiable clause for divorce? Because marriage is a representation of Christ and the church, and unrepentant sexual sin is an attack on that image. Inasmuch, *all* unrepentant sin is an attack on the cross. How can you claim to love Christ and be unrepentantly unfaithful to Him? What kind of Messiah is Christ if He is unfaithful to His church and breaks His promises? Nevertheless, we are to forgive those who wronged us. If your spouse repents of their sin, even sexual sin, how can you claim to be Christlike by divorcing them?

Furthermore, Paul would later give another reason for divorce and remarriage. 1 Corinthians 7: 12-16 says, "But to the rest *I say, not the Lord,* that if any brother has an unbelieving wife, and she consents to live with him, he must not divorce her. And if any woman has an unbelieving husband, and he consents to live with her, she must not divorce her husband. For the unbelieving husband is sanctified through his wife, and the unbelieving wife is sanctified through her believing husband; for otherwise your children are unclean, but now they are holy. Yet *if* the unbelieving one is leaving, let him leave; the brother or the sister is *not under bondage* in such cases, but God has called us in peace. For how do you know, wife, whether you will save your husband? Or how do you know, husband, whether you will save your wife?"

Paul is saying that even if a Christian has an unbelieving spouse, if that spouse wants to remain married, then the Christian is not to divorce them. However, if the unbelieving spouse wants to leave, let them leave; the Christian is not bound in such a circumstance. Why? Because unrepentant unbelief is an attack on the cross. You can't be part of the church and remain in unbelief.

However, does that mean an unbeliever is forbidden to come to church? Absolutely not! However, if that unbeliever doesn't respect the guidelines of the church, we are to remove that person from the church. Why? For we are to do the same thing even with those who call themselves believers!

Jesus says in Matthew 18: 15-17, "Now if your brother sins, go and show him his fault in private; if he listens to you, you have gained your brother. But if he does not listen to you, take one or two more with you, so that ON THE TESTIMONY OF TWO OR THREE WITNESSES EVERY MATTER MAY BE CONFIRMED. And if he refuses to listen to them, tell it to the church; and if he refuses to listen even to the church, he is to be to you as a Gentile and a tax collector."

If someone who claims to be a Christian is living in unrepentant sin and refuses to be instructed by the church, the church is to regard that person as an unbeliever. Furthermore, 1 Timothy 5:8 says, "But if *anyone* does not provide for his own, and especially for those of his household, he has denied the faith and is *worse* than an unbeliever." Meaning, even if a man calls himself a Christian, if he refuses to do his job as a husband, then he has denied the faith and is *worse* than an unbeliever. And if someone *worse* than an unbeliever wants to leave, then *I* would say, "Let them leave. You are not bound to such a circumstance." For if *I* was married and my wife was living in unrepentant sin after multiple rebukes, I would give her two options, saying, "It's either me or the sin. You can't have both." And if she chooses the sin, it isn't me she's rejecting, but Christ, for she has denied Him with her actions.

Which is why I say divorce and remarriage is an attack on the cross (if taken lightly). The question the Pharisees asked Jesus was "Is it *lawful*?" However, as mentioned when talking about women being leaders and teachers of men, there are circumstances in which divorce and remarriage is allowed, but it should always be a last resort. Even so, ask yourself this question: "If I am to be conformed to the image of Christ, and Jesus commands me to love others as He loved us (John 13:34), what would I do if I was in the process of exchanging vows to the person I hoped to marry and my ex-spouse came and interrupted the ceremony asking for forgiveness and reconciliation?" Let it sink in.

This is why it's important for those who have never been married to be conformed to the image of Christ beforehand. However, many who seek to be married, even amongst Christians, fall into the same trap as the false-teachers. That being, they desire the protection from pain and the pursuit of pleasure. They desire safety and security.

If you want to be married, and God only gives good gifts to His children, honestly ask yourself: "Would *I* be a good gift for His child?" For there are plenty of men who are looking for a good wife, but don't know what it means to be a good husband, and there are plenty of women looking for a good husband, but don't know what it means to be a good wife. Why? Because all the attributes an individual needs to be a good *spouse* are the same attributes an individual needs to be a good *person*! And most people don't know what it means to be a good person. Meaning, if you don't know how to *be* a good person, you don't know how to *find* a good person.

Romans 12: 2-3 says, "Do not *conform* to the pattern of this world, but be *transformed* by the renewing of your mind. Then you will be able to test and approve what God's will is—his good, pleasing and perfect will. For by the grace given me I say to every one of you: Do not think of yourself more highly than you ought, but rather think of yourself with sober judgment, in accordance with the faith God has distributed to each of you." (NIV)

Inasmuch, if you don't have a heart and lifestyle that's transformed by Christ, you will hope to find someone who is going to meet all your worldly desires, not someone who is going to help you meet your Heavenly calling. I can't tell you how many women I met online, even "devout" Christian women, who didn't understand this. They may have had "Christian" in the religion column, but their entire sense of worth was wrapped up in something other than Christ, and with most of them I was able to figure that out just by their profiles. If your profile is supposed to be your best foot forward, being carefully crafted and communicated for its greatest impact, then what is a good man (i.e., a good person) supposed to be impressed by?

"I went to *this* college. I majored in *this* field. I work at *this* company. I have *this* position. I eat *this* particular diet. I have *this* particular workout schedule. I have *this* particular hobby. I travel *this* many times a year. I travel to *these* particular places. I do *these* particular things while I'm there. I have *this* many kids. I have *this* many pets. I have hardly any free time due to my schedule, so I'm looking for someone who does all the same things and perfectly fits my schedule, or else we won't have time for each other."

Some of the women who were feeling extra Christian would add, "I'm of *this* denomination. *This* is my favorite verse. *This* is my opinion on God or the Bible." To which, it was often something naive or heretical. (In fairness, I'm certain most men's profiles were of the same sort. But the question remains: "What does any of that have to do with being a good person?")

However, there was a common theme I would read: "I believe it's the man's job to pursue the woman. To which, *you* would have to forsake whatever *you* have going on and move to where *I* am and conform to *my* schedule." Even though what I had going on at the time wasn't the most impressive by worldly standards, I was fully convinced I was where God wanted me to be and to remain for the foreseeable future. However, even if I was higher on the socioeconomic ladder with lots of flexibility, I still would have been alarmed by these profiles, if not completely put off.

Yes, for this reason a man shall leave father and mother, to be joined with his wife and the two shall become one flesh. However, these women forget what Paul says in 1 Corinthians 11: 8-9, "Man does not originate from woman, but woman from man; <u>for indeed man was not created for the woman's sake, but woman for the man's sake.</u>" Meaning, Adam wasn't made to be Eve's helper, but Eve was made to be Adam's helper. That is not to say a man can't be willingly flexible, but that when push comes to shove, the husband has the final word.

However, as 1 Peter 3:7 points out, husbands are to consider their wives' desires in the same manner they hope Christ will be considerate of their own prayers. Headship and dictatorship are not synonymous, and neither is submission and passivity. If your husband is asking you to sin, don't do it. Submit yourselves *as unto the Lord*. To which, the Lord will not ask you to sin.

Nevertheless, for some of us, it's already "too late" and we're stuck in a miserable marriage. The husband doesn't want to lead, or the wife doesn't want to submit. They may not be abusive or negligent, but they won't live up to the potential inside of them, or they won't let us live up to our own potential. What are we to do?

Granted, I'm not married, but if I was in such a marriage, I would have this approach: Innocent as a dove but shrewd as a viper. If you can't convince them to live up to your standards for Christ honoring reasons, then convince them to do so for practical reasons. I mean, what would you do to get what you wanted from an over-bearing boss, a disagreeable neighbor, or even a thief pointing a gun at your head? Furthermore, there is a way to do so and not argue. I shall explain.

You don't necessarily have to convince people into giving you what you want in order to get what you want. In fact, it's usually easier to mislead people by convincing them the way to go about getting what *they* want involves methods that in fact result in giving *you* what *you* want.

For example: You're hitchhiking in the passenger seat of someone else's car and you want to go east, but the driver wants to go west. You don't have to convince the driver to go east, you just have to convince him the direction he is going is west, when in fact, he's going east. That's why selfish and power-hungry people don't teach you *how* to think, but *what* to think. For if they taught you *how* to think, then you would have the ability to recognize what they're up to and you won't go in the direction they are wanting you to go.

The point being, there are "methods" and there are "results". Don't waste time trying to convince them to simply give you what you want as the "result", but convince them that what you want is the method which results in them getting something *they* want. And in my experience, women are much better at this than men are, although women are more likely to pursue methods that are in the vein of "better to receive forgiveness than permission". That being, instead of waiting for the husband's approval, they go ahead and get what they want behind the husband's back and hope he will feel too guilty to make her give it back. But such methods are not respectful, and they tend to result in the husband being resentful.

Jesus said in Matthew 13:44, "The kingdom of heaven is like a treasure hidden in the field, which a man found and hid again; and from joy over it he goes and sells everything that he has, and buys that field." That being, no one gives up what they have unless they're convinced that something else is better. Unfortunately, most people try to have the best of both worlds. They want to have their cake and eat it too. They want to serve two masters instead of one.

But Jesus says in Luke 16:13, "No servant can serve two masters; for either he will hate the one and love the other, or he will be devoted to one and despise the other. You cannot serve God and wealth." Inasmuch, you can't have your cake and eat it too. You can't pursue righteousness and unrighteousness at the same time. You can't love God and hate Him at the same time.

All in all, we are not only to honor Christ in our marriages, but in our lives. I'm not saying to give up your career and take up a humbler profession. As mentioned, it's better to be rich and grateful than to be poor and self-righteous or grumbling. I'm not saying to forsake your hobbies, for we all need a break from the daily grind of life every now and then. I'm simply saying that if the crux of your life is to protect yourself from pain and to pursue pleasure wherever you can find it, then you will never live your life to the fullest, and you have probably yet to receive life eternal.

Furthermore, being able to answer every question during Sunday school and volunteering to stack chairs afterwards doesn't make you a good person worthy of receiving a spouse, or *anything* else, for that matter. I had to learn that the hard way. Also, not getting the outcome I desired from such wisdom and chivalry made me resentful, and that unresolved resentfulness led me to find sinful methods to vent my frustrations; creating a vicious cycle that left me perpetually single and miserable.

However, Jesus said in Mark 11: 24-26, "Therefore, I say to you, all things for which you pray and ask, believe that you have received them, and they will be granted to you. And whenever you stand praying, forgive, if you have anything against anyone, so that your Father who is in heaven will also forgive you for your offenses. But if you do not forgive, neither will your Father who is in heaven forgive your offenses." Inasmuch, if you're harboring unforgiveness towards another person, then God will not answer your prayers. For if you feel resentment towards another person, it means one of two things: You either need to grow up, or stand up.

What do I mean? By "grow up", I mean you need to stop being so petty, emotionally fragile, bitter, unable to take a joke, a criticism, or a rejection, so as to cause a rift between you and another person. By "stand up", I mean you need to learn how to stand up for yourself and let it be known to your offender that you resent (yet forgive) what they are doing to you or have done to you, whether it be abuse, neglect, taking advantage, being annoying, or whatever else that inconveniences you. If the thing which is making you resentful is an actual sin against you, and you are to forgive them, then surely you are to get over an inconvenience or at least tell the person that what they are doing is bothering you.

As James 4: 1-3 says, "What is the source of quarrels and conflicts among you [or *within* you]? Is the source not your pleasures that wage war in your body's parts? You lust and do not have, so you commit murder. And you are envious and cannot obtain, so you fight and quarrel [even within yourself]. You do not have because you do not ask. You ask and do not receive, because you ask with the wrong motives, so that you may spend what you request on your pleasures."

If you don't know how to grow up or to stand up for yourself, why should God give you a gift of any kind? For you will either use that gift for revenge or to at least puff yourself up in the eyes of others, or you will be unable to stand up to your oppressor when they demand that you give them the gift. Or, you will at least be unable to stand up for yourself in a righteous or healthy manner. If you can't handle rejection (or rather, if you can't handle being the kind of person of whom no one in their right mind would want to reject) then you can't handle that which you want to receive. For even if you received it, you wouldn't know what to do with it should it not function the way you hoped it would. Inasmuch, spouses tend to have a mind of their own.

Nevertheless, being rejected by a love interest is not synonymous with being sinned against. Even if they were to laugh at you for even thinking you had a chance, you are to forgive them. Also, any self-justifying sentiments of "Well, if that's their reaction, they clearly aren't as mature and spiritual as *I* am! To which, good riddance!" I can almost assure you that if such a sentiment is your natural knee-jerk reaction, then you're not as mature and spiritual as you think you are. For if you were as in-tune with the

Holy Spirit as you think you were, then you would have recognized that the love interest wasn't worthy of being a love interest before professing your love to them. Or, worse yet, that they were indeed worthy of affection, but *you*, in fact, were not. For many people can handle being called crazy, stupid, or evil, but not many can handle being be called "unworthy". Criticism is a tough pill to swallow, but pride is a tougher pill.

CULTURE VS COUNTER-CULTURE

If you're not being transformed by the renewing of your mind, then you're being conformed to the pattern of this world. And the pattern of this world is this: My personal happiness is the number one priority in my life and no one is to intrude on my happiness. Even if you don't want that happiness to be found in sex or marriage, you still want to have it.

However, many people pursue other pleasures simply because they can't acquire sex or marriage. That being, if they want to be happy in sex or marriage, but can't attain it, then they must find another way to find happiness. To which, they get caught up in their career or hobbies. Perhaps they start collecting toys and tools, or even help others to acquire the very things they can't acquire for themselves. Inasmuch, if they are to be happy at all, it is to see other people being happy. Even so, after a while, it weighs heavily on the soul. Meanwhile, there are those who simply "have it all" when it comes to the pleasures of this world. That being, they have marriage, sex, money, status, popularity, etc.

However, in Ecclesiastes, Solomon writes as through the perspective of there being no God. That being, he writes as though there is no hope. Solomon was the wisest man to ever live before Christ, and yet, he claimed that his attempt to find meaning in knowledge left him feeling empty. Solomon had 700 wives and 300 concubines, and yet, he claimed that finding meaning in pleasure left him unsatisfied. Solomon was one of the richest kings ever, and yet, he said the pursuit of wealth was hollow. Vanity, vanity, all is vanity. All is striving after the wind if without God.

Yet, there are plenty who pursue such things and do indeed feel satisfied. To which, I would say they haven't pursued knowledge, sex, or wealth to the fullest, or else they would come to the same conclusion. That being, even in the pursuit of knowledge, sex, and wealth, something else is a greater priority which holds them back. Perhaps it's their family, fear of failure, or even their conscience. Inasmuch, they still find their sense of meaning and purpose in something other than God.

However, God is the source of all meaning and purpose. If there is no God, then the universe has no meaning and purpose. If life is a product of the universe, then life has no meaning and purpose. And if life has no meaning and purpose, then there is not a manner of life in which we are meant to live or that gives us purpose. Any sense of meaning and purpose is a trick that evolution pulls on us to keep us from despair, depression, and suicide. For you can't reproduce the species if you're too lazy, unimpressive, or dead.

If there is no God, any hope to be found in religion is a fool's hope. And even if there is a God, if He requires worship, and we don't worship Him in an acceptable manner, if at all, then whatever else we are worshiping is false worship. Inasmuch, false worship is false hope.

Some atheists claim that religion was a method weak people used against the strong to get the results they wanted. That being, in a time when "physical might equals morally right", those who were weak had to find a way to not be oppressed. To which, they invented religion to scare the strong into obeying them. Or, it provided some kind of comfort that if they suffer in this life, they will have a better life after death. Some say that Christianity itself was a way for the oppressed to get back at their oppressors. They say Christianity praises charity for the sake of the rich giving to the poor. Or, that forgiveness is morally superior to revenge; a notion to make them feel better for being too powerless to achieve revenge.

However, why would Christians, who hope to overcome their oppressors, come up with a religion that commands *everyone* to follow such guidelines? Why would they come up with a religion that teaches, "If your neighbor forces you to go one mile, go two miles. If your neighbor strikes you on the right cheek, turn to him the other also. If your neighbor sues you for your coat, don't withhold your shirt. If anyone denies Me before men, I will deny Him before My Father in Heaven. Whoever seeks to save their life will lose it, but whoever loses their life for My sake will find it."?

If Christianity was invented by the weak to empower the weak, it did a terrible job. Yes, Christianity eventually became the dominant religion through Constantine, but many Christians suffered and died for their faith before then. Yes, Christianity was then used to oppress non-Christians, but oppressing and killing others in the name of Christianity goes against what Christ taught. To which, why would Constantine and the Council of Nicaea "invent" a religion that condemns such notions? (Granted, many of the founding fathers of the United States declared "All men are created equal and have the right to life, liberty, and the pursuit of happiness" while owning slaves.)

Nevertheless, such teachings strike right at the heart of personal happiness, don't they? So, why do we listen to a culture that says, "Happiness is the truth"? Furthermore, why should we cater to such a God-hating and self-exalting culture? We preach a Gospel that commands everyone everywhere to humble themselves and repent, not tell them that God accepts them just the way they are.

For Romans 1: 16-32 says, "For <u>I am not ashamed of the gospel, for it is the power of God for salvation to everyone who believes,</u> to the Jew first and also to the Greek. For in it the righteousness of God is revealed from faith to faith; as it is written: 'BUT THE RIGHTEOUS ONE WILL LIVE BY FAITH.'

<u>For the wrath of God is revealed from heaven against all ungodliness and unrighteousness of people who *suppress the truth in unrighteousness*, because that which is *known* about God is *evident* within them; for *God made it evident to them*. For since the creation of the world His invisible attributes, that is, His eternal power and divine nature, have been *clearly perceived*, being *understood* by what has been made, so that *they are without excuse.*</u> For even though they *knew* God, they did not honor Him as God or give thanks, but they became futile in their reasonings, and their senseless hearts were darkened. <u>Claiming to be wise, they became fools</u>, and they exchanged the glory of the incorruptible God for an image in the form of corruptible mankind, of birds, four-footed animals, and crawling creatures.

Therefore, God gave them up to vile impurity in the lusts of their hearts, so that their bodies would be dishonored among them. For <u>they exchanged the truth of God for falsehood, and worshiped and served the creature rather than the Creator</u>, who is blessed forever. Amen.

For this reason, God gave them over to degrading passions; for their women exchanged natural relations for that which is contrary to nature, and likewise the men, too, abandoned natural relations with women and <u>burned in their desire toward one another</u>, males with males committing shameful acts and receiving in their own persons the due penalty of their error.

<u>And just as they did not see fit to acknowledge God, God gave them up to a depraved mind, to do those things that are not</u>

<u>proper</u>, people having been filled with all unrighteousness, wickedness, greed, and evil; full of envy, murder, strife, deceit, and malice; they are gossips, slanderers, <u>haters of God</u>, insolent, arrogant, boastful, <u>inventors of evil</u>, disobedient to parents, without understanding, untrustworthy, unfeeling, and unmerciful; <u>and although they _know_ the ordinance of God, that those who practice such things are worthy of _death_, they not only do the same, but also approve of those who practice them_</u>."

If God does not approve of their behavior, then neither should we. All who unrepentantly practice such things are under God's wrath, not His love. If they are under His love at all, it is the fact that God has yet to exact justice and kill them. Any misery they suffer in this life is still to be considered a blessing, given they still have a life and a chance to repent. And if you call yourself a Christian, and yet, approve of any of the behaviors mentioned, how can you claim to have a right relationship with God? And if you don't have a right relationship with God, you are under His wrath; not His love. Repent!

However, that brings us back to homosexuality. For there are plenty of Christians who denounce everything on that list, except for homosexuality. Some same-sex apologists claim that what is being condemned in Romans 1 is heterosexual men and women doing what is unnatural for them by engaging in homosexual acts, not homosexuality in itself. That being, it's a sin for a straight man to have sex with another man, and a straight woman to have sex with another woman. In turn, it would be a sin for a gay man to have sex with a woman and for a gay woman to have sex with a man. Inasmuch, in their minds, it isn't a condemnation against same-sex marriage.

Here's the problem with that logic: Heterosexual people do not _burn in desire_ for the same sex. And as explained in the previous chapter, all sexual sin is an attack on the cross. How can you submit to Christ, and yet, be hostile towards what He represents? How can you be part of the church, and yet, despise the role of the church?

You cannot serve two masters. In this case, we can't serve Christ and the Christ-hating culture. We cannot hope to change the culture by catering to it. If so, we haven't won the culture, for it has won us. God sent a flood to judge the world for its sin, and gave us the rainbow as a sign that He would never flood the earth again. Now, the rainbow is a banner that celebrates the very kinds of sins that God sent a flood to judge the world in the first place.

What I find somewhat amusing is the in-fighting that goes on amongst those in the LGBTQ+ movement. For one thing, it started as LGB, then they added T, then the Q, and then gave up and added a + to include anything else that came after that. Furthermore, there are conflicting worldviews within the LGBTQ+ that cause friction. There are plenty among Lesbians, Gays, and Bisexuals who don't think any of the other letters should be part of their group, saying the others should have their own group.

They say, "The Transgender community is something different than ourselves. We're not concerned with our sexual identity, but with our sexual attraction. We're completely comfortable with our genders in the traditional or biological sense." Furthermore, there are Lesbians, Gays, and Bisexuals, who deny that Transgender people are even *sane*, claiming they have a mental disorder or are only seeking attention. Many are also horrified of how Transgenderism is being pushed onto children. (Not to mention there are talks about adding a P for Pedophilia.)

On the other hand, there are those among the other letters and activists who hate Transgenders because they affirm that there are only two genders! They say, "Gender is fluid!" and such people often call themselves "non-binary". That being, they don't claim to be a man or a woman. But even then, to say you are non-binary is to ignore all the other "sexes" that aren't male or female! As Romans 1 says, God gave them over to a depraved mind. They have become futile in their speculations, or in this case, in their declarations. They are inventors of evil without understanding, and they are quite unmerciful towards their opposition.

As far as whether or not we should refer to people by their preferred pronouns or names, I leave that to your own personal conscience. I heard plenty of people say they were going keep saying "Bruce Jenner" instead of "Caitlyn Jenner", but didn't have a second thought in saying "Chaz Bono" instead of "Chasity Bono". We have no problem saying Puff Daddy, P Diddy, or Diddy. So, where is the line drawn as to how far we can entertain someone's ego?

However, that is not to say we are to remain silent when it comes to such issues. Whether or not we should call someone a he, she, it, they, them, etc. is different than actually affirming that there are more than two sexes or that one sex can become another sex. For God made them male and female. Even if you were born with an extra chromosome, your genitalia should be an easy clue to figure out which sex you should live as. As for hermaphrodites, there is no Biblical or Scriptural reference of them, much less any instruction for them. I would leave that as a matter of conscience, as well.

[Disclaimer: Unfortunately, the data on the following statistics is highly suppressed by the media and I can no longer find an actual "source" for a citation. All the websites available only spoke about LGBTQ+ suicide *attempts*, didn't compare the suicide rates to other demographics, or didn't discuss LGBTQ+ suicide rates at all. Furthermore, almost all who did have information blamed bullying or lack of support as the main reason for suicide, if not the sole reason. To which, the following is merely my own opinion based on memory that may not be 100% verifiable and I apologize for any misinformation.]

(If memory serves) Transgender people have the highest suicide rate in the country, with military veterans having the second-highest rate. In *No Filter*, I discussed my own attempt at suicide and what I have learned about the subject. I have learned that no one takes their life while clinging to the hope that there is another way of escaping their misery, unless it is purely out of spite. Although, like a defeated Samurai, some might commit suicide from a sense of honor.

Yet, why is it that military veterans commit suicide at a lesser rate than transgenders? Why does either group want to commit suicide at all? <u>My *theory*</u>: Feelings of alienation/disassociation. If there is a worse feeling in the world than being alone, it is to still feel alone when surrounded by people. Inasmuch, to have an inescapable feeling of something being wrong or out of place can drive you insane, even if there is no evidence for it other than your feelings.

With military veterans suffering from PTSD (Post-Traumatic Stress Disorder), many of them find relief from their symptoms if they reenlist into the military. Or, some find relief when a disaster situation takes place, such as 9/11 or Hurricane Katrina. I know of a former soldier with PTSD who is not only married with multiple children, but has since gotten multiple dogs, multiple cats, and works as a veterinarian. When asked why he would do that to himself, he said, "I need the chaos. If everything was simple, I would start going crazy. I need the distraction."

Inasmuch, many veterans who suffer from PTSD can find relief if they find a way to distract themselves, or to find another sense of purpose other than being a soldier. The feelings of alienation and disassociation can be suppressed if they are put in a different situation. However, *true* transgenders, not those who call themselves transgender for the sake of attention, have a worse problem: They feel alienated or disassociated within their own skin. And unlike a former-soldier, there is no situation in which they can escape from themselves.

(If memory serves) The suicide rate for those who have yet to transition to their preferred sex is lower than those who have transitioned. Perhaps it is because those who have yet to transition are still clinging to the hope that the transition will solve their problems, whereas those who have transitioned are now left with no excuse for their misery. But for those who have yet to transition, and yet, still commit suicide, they might have come to the conclusion that even a transition wouldn't solve their problems, or there was a different underlying problem that manifested itself in the pursuit of being transgender.

This isn't a problem only transgenders face. Although they struggle with the concept of "God making them male or female", anyone who struggles with the concept of being "made in the image of God" is going to face an identity crisis, as well. I remember a story on *Ripley's Believe It or Not* about a Native-American man named Dennis Avner "Stalking Cat" who was convinced he needed to become a cat and received plastic surgery to make himself look like a tiger. Unfortunately, he committed suicide in September 2007. Whether or not his suicide was due to him regretting becoming a tiger, or feeling that becoming a tiger was unattainable, can't be determined. However, we can say the same about transgender people who commit suicide. Correlation doesn't necessarily mean causation, but it correlates too often to be ignored. (Also, Native-Americans have the highest national suicide rate according to race and ethnicity, according to the CDC)

Nevertheless, there are plenty of people within the LGBTQ+ movement who are wanting attention. Why would I say such a thing? For 1 in 6 people in Generation Z (People born roughly between 1995 and 2015) identify as LGBTQ+, as compared to 1 in 40 Millennials (people born roughly between 1981 and 1995). Inasmuch, every generation is more perverse, or at least, confused, than the previous generation. People may argue that Generation Z is more open and honest about their sexuality than Millennials because we are more tolerant today than we were before. However, if such is the case, then wouldn't more and more Millennials be "coming out of the closet" and bring the 1:40 ratio closer to the 1:6 ratio?

If these sexual identities are completely natural and universal, then so should be the ratio. If the degree of tolerance today towards the LGBTQ+ community is allowing people to be "honest with themselves", then why the disparity between the two generations? It's either because:

1) Millennials are still willing to keep their private lives private

2) Generation Z feels a greater need to broadcast their true sexuality

3) Generation Z feels a greater need to lie about their true sexuality for the sake of gaining attention and not being a boring Cisgender.

4) All of the above.

However, groups 2 and 3 have the same problem, in that both groups feel the need to draw attention to themselves for one reason or another. Inasmuch, those within groups 1 and 2 tend to be more willing to have civil dialog, whether it be in private or public. However, Group 3 tends to be uncivil in private as well as public. They get upset at people for not using their preferred pronouns the same way a woman dressed like a stripper gets upset at men who have a hard time keeping their eyes to themselves. If you don't want the attention, then why create such a visual? If you don't want to cause trouble, why throw a temper tantrum?

Furthermore, they don't just throw a temper tantrum when someone like myself "assumes" them to be a man, despite them having a beard and penis, but they throw a temper tantrum when a Cisgendered man like myself refuses to date them. For those of you who are out of the loop, a Cisgendered man is a biologically born man who is completely comfortable that way and is only attracted to biologically born women (aka what was formerly and simply known as "heterosexual"). Inasmuch, calling someone Cisgender is typically meant to be an insult by such people.

Such people often say that I, a Cisgendered man, am not to condemn a homosexual man for being attracted to another man, for he was born that way and can't help but to be attracted to who he is attracted to. Yet, such people also typically say we should live our lives however we want without judgement or interference. However, if we are free to live our lives however we want, why should it matter whether the homosexual chooses to be a homosexual or not? If I can't condemn someone for living their life however they want, then I shouldn't be able to condemn a man who *chooses* to live a homosexual lifestyle, regardless of his true sexual attractions. Meaning, whether or not a man chooses to be homosexual or can't help but to be homosexual, I can't condemn him, according to liberal logic.

However, somehow, also according to liberal logic, I as a "Cisgendered man" am expected to ignore or overcome my natural inclinations a date someone I don't want to date, or else I'm a bigot of the worse kind and deserve all the vitriol of hell. These are often the same people who claim that an unwanted hand on the shoulder is equivalent to rape, but, somehow, forcing me to have a romantic relationship with someone I don't want to have a relationship with is "progress". Right...

Nevertheless, one of the main driving factors in the LGBTQ+ community, and even the feminist community, is to push against the rigid societal norms and forging their own path. Inasmuch, the previous generation was 1:40, and the current generation is 1:6. Thus, we can suppose that the next generation will be more or less 1:1, and the following generation will be even further, possibly tipping the scales at 6:1, and the generation after that will be 40:1. Meaning, in the next few generations, the Cisgendered will be the oppressed minority. The Cisgendered will be pushing against the societal norms. The Cisgendered will be forging their own path. [Thus, I'm not a bigot, but a prophet. I'm not behind the times, but ahead of my time.]

On the other hand, the transgender movement flies in the face of the feminist movement. Feminism started out as a movement in which women would be able to have an equal voice to men when it came to politics and the work place. At first, feminists partnered with Christians in the pursuit of ridding the world of pornography. However, at some point, a new wave of feminists thought that pornography was empowering for women, for it allowed women to express their sexuality in a way that didn't conform to traditional family norms.

Feminism used to say companies should hire more women, given that women can offer a unique perspective. Now, many want to claim there are no differences in men and women at all; that a woman can do anything a man can do to the same degree. Even so, whether or not there are differences is dependent on whether or not it helps their argument when it comes to getting what they want. To which, such ideologies have paved the way for the LGBTQ+ movement to take things even further, to the point where transgender women (men who "became women") are competing in women's sports and breaking all the records.

Ironically, there are some among the transgender community who want to also claim there are no differences between men and women, and that all differences are socially constructed. If such is the case, then why do men feel like women or women feel like men? If there's no difference, then you shouldn't feel a difference. How would you even know the difference? Furthermore, why bother changing the sex on your ID from M to F or F to M? Why not simply leave it blank? Why bother with surgery? Why bother with anything?

Nevertheless, whether you want to be called a man or a woman, to wear pants or a dress, to get surgery or remain as you are, the problem remains: You will never be able to hide from, escape from, or overcome the fact that you are still you.

However, when it comes to feminists, no matter what wave of feminism they claim to be, they're almost always Pro-Choice. It's one thing when the God-hating world advocates for abortion, but it's another thing to hear those within the church advocating for abortion. Not only that, but I heard one person claim that the right to abortion was a "Gospel issue". Meaning, Christ wants us to have the right to abort our children. For they too are deceived by the lie that the Gospel proclaims Christ died for our happiness. But abortion is an attack on the Gospel, not a display of it.

The Gospel is that Jesus, an innocent person, willingly gave His life for the sake of His enemy's sins to allow them to have the eternal life they didn't deserve. Abortion is a sinful woman killing her innocent child for the sake of allowing her to have the life she *thinks* she deserves. If abortion is symbolized by the Gospel, it's represented by those who nailed Jesus to the cross.

Furthermore, there is no such thing as "life-saving abortion". If a woman's life is in danger while going into labor, an emergency C-section can be performed in 15 minutes. An abortion at that stage takes two days of preparation, and the medication would put her life at even greater risk because it drops her blood pressure.

Abortion clinics around the country claim abortion is a matter of women's health. If such is the case, then wouldn't it be much safer for the abortion doctor to use an ultrasound to see what he is doing? However, many, if not most abortion clinics, don't even offer ultrasounds. But why? Former abortion clinicians claim, "Because most women don't go through with an abortion after seeing an ultrasound of the baby. Although we offered other services than abortion, most of our money came from abortions. If most women didn't go through with the abortion, it would have been financially disastrous."

There are some abortion advocates who are truly deceived in thinking it's a matter of women's health, but everyone who has thought it through knows it's truly about the money and independence. It's no different than the days of idolatry, when people would sacrifice their children to gods. They sacrificed their children to the gods of Safety and Security, and nothing has changed. The only difference is we now cut out the middle man by doing away with religious practices and resort to more secular methods and reasons. Nevertheless, there were Israelites in the times of the prophets who saw no problem with sacrificing their children, so we shouldn't be surprised there are "Christians" today who feel the same.

Matthew 15: 1-9 says, "Then some Pharisees and scribes came to Jesus from Jerusalem and said, 'Why do Your disciples break the tradition of the elders? For they do not wash their hands when they eat bread.' And He answered and said to them, 'Why do you yourselves also break the commandment of God for the sake of your tradition? For God said, 'HONOR YOUR FATHER AND MOTHER,' and, 'THE ONE WHO SPEAKS EVIL OF FATHER OR MOTHER IS TO BE PUT TO DEATH.' But *you* say, 'Whoever says to his father or mother, 'Whatever I have that would help you has been given to God,' he is not to honor his father or mother.' And by this you have invalidated the word of God for the sake of your tradition. You hypocrites, rightly did Isaiah prophesy about you, by saying: 'THIS PEOPLE HONORS ME WITH THEIR LIPS, BUT THEIR HEART IS FAR AWAY FROM ME.' 'AND IN VAIN DO THEY WORSHIP ME, TEACHING AS DOCTRINES THE COMMANDMENTS OF MEN.'''

The Pharisees were claiming, for example, that if a man's parents said, "We need this goat," but the man says, "I'm going to sacrifice it to God," then the man doesn't have to honor his father and mother. Such a teaching was one the Pharisees invented and expected others to follow, and claimed those who disobeyed it were actually disobeying God. But Jesus said such a mindset was evil.

In the case of abortion, do you think you could get away with saying, "I'm going to sacrifice this child for the sake of being free to serve the Lord!" Of course, not! For in doing so you would be breaking the commandment "You shall not murder". If you are not allowed to have an abortion for the sake of being free to spread the Gospel to the ends of the earth, then there's no circumstance in which it's permitted. Whether or not abortion should be *legal* in the *country* is one thing, but to say it should be *celebrated* among the *church* is truly of Satan.

Fortunately, we serve such a God in which no matter how many abortions you've had, or how many abortions you've performed, there is forgiveness for anyone who truly repents. If the Apostle Paul could spend three years of his life killing Christians, and yet, be transformed and used by God in such a mighty way, then so can you or anyone else. Today, if you hear His voice, do not harden your heart. (And if you would like to receive counseling or to help prevent abortion, visit preborn.org)

However, this is where Counter-Culture comes in. For there are many among the Christian right-wing conservatives who plead with those who are seeking abortion to put their children up for adoption. Here's the problem: There are about 437,000 children in foster care every year in the United States. However, only 2% of Americans have actually adopted, and they only adopt 135,000 children every year. Furthermore, out of those 135,000 children, only 74% (99,900) were from the United States, and the other 26% (35,100) were from abroad. And lastly, there were 862,320 *abortions* in 2017.

If all the children who were aborted were put up for adoption instead, the number of children in foster care would go from 437,000 to 1,300,000. If only about 100,000 American children are adopted every year, that would still leave 1,200,000 children in American foster care, and the foster care system is under-staffed and underfunded already. Meaning, we need to do more than simply trying to convince them to put their children up for adoption or to practice abstinence.

The problem lies in the fact that, for the most part, right-wing conservatives are all show and no substance. They focus more on providing a counter argument to the culture rather than actually coming up with real solutions. Not only that, but they typically want to deny that the problems liberals hope to solve are actually problems, or at least problems worthy of consideration. Inasmuch, dealing with those problems would distract from their own selfish goals as conservatives. For they too have bought into the lie that safety, security, and personal happiness is the most important factor of their lives.

I picture the dilemma between liberals and conservatives like this: Liberals are a starved-for-attention teenage girl who wants to go to a party with her friends because they'll be some boys there, and conservatives are an emotionally unavailable father who is always too busy to be bothered. The father makes a fairly convincing argument as to why the party is a bad idea, but when the daughter asks for an alternative, the father says, "Not now, I'm busy. Go do your homework or something." In so doing, he callously disregards the daughter's emotional needs for his own selfish ambition in the name of taking up personal responsibility.

Inasmuch, the daughter has now grown up, and she doesn't take too kindly to being ignored by *anyone*, or else "You're just like my father!" What we now call the Woke Culture is hypersensitive to anything that could be deemed racist, sexist, homophobic, etc. and is quick to boycott and protest. Such actions have given rise to what I call the Anti-Woke Culture/Movement, which is hypersensitive to anything that could be deemed "Woke". The Woke Culture is hypersensitive whenever a minority isn't represented in art and industry, and the Anti-Woke Culture is hypersensitive whenever there *is* a minority represented in art and industry. Inasmuch, the father is now raging at his daughter, saying, "After all the hard work to put a roof over your head, *this* is the thanks I get?"

However, there are those who identify as liberal who are among the Anti-Woke. For I have seen plenty of liberal comedians who are hostile towards the Woke, and I find the jokes that ensue quite amusing, if I'm being honest. For the best comedians are those who are willing to call out nonsense for what it is, no matter which side of the political/religious spectrum the comedian leans towards.

On the other hand, I don't know of any *political* conservatives who are Woke, but I have seen many *evangelicals* become Woke over the years. And in many cases, they're among the worst of Belials. For there are plenty of Belials who claim "the Holy Spirit" tells them something different than Scripture, but Woke Belials claim "Culture" tells them something different. At least Spirit Belials are still exercising a form of religiosity, but Woke Belials are exercising cultural conformity.

Why? Because the church is slowly buying into the Satanic lie that loving your neighbor as yourself means to be nice to everyone no matter who they are or what they're doing. However, if the God-hating world is at peace with you, it's because you're not living out and preaching the Gospel message. The same Jesus who cautioned us against passing judgement also said in the same breath to not give what is holy to dogs or cast our pearls before pigs. The same Jesus who told us to love our enemies also called His enemies a brood of vipers, sons of the devil, jackals, hypocrites, etc. The same Jesus that told us to be innocent as doves also said to be shrewd as vipers.

If your idea of living out the Christian life is to make non-Christians comfortable around us, how then do you expect the non-Christian world to be convicted of their sin so as to repent? If there are parts of the Bible that make *you* uncomfortable, especially to the point of refusing to talk about it, how then do you expect non-Christians to think the Bible is worth following? If we want to see the world transformed, we ourselves must be transformed. When the world looks at us and says, "You're different than me," it should be for a reason greater than simply having a different opinion than themselves.

Yet, even if they're convinced that we practice what we preach, they won't necessarily be convinced that what we preach is worth practicing. That being, if we respond to the least bit of persecution by acting just as chaotically, if not more so, than the rest of the world, how then will the Christian life be a better alternative?

The world reacts hysterically when their beliefs are challenged because they're convinced their very identity and source of happiness is under threat, whether they're Woke or Anti-Woke. If the world is going to let go of the world, it won't be through a mere statement of facts that proves their worldview to be nonsensical, if not dangerous. Furthermore, it won't be by having those facts angrily shouted at them. If the world responds to feelings and not facts, then all they pay attention to is the anger when you shout "Facts don't care about your feelings!"

One of the biggest reasons Donald Trump won the election in 2016 was for his unapologetic approach when it came to debating his opponents. However, it wasn't so much that he was speaking facts, but that he was brutal and insulting with his choice of vocabulary, and for that reason, he was loved by the Anti-Woke conservatives. He was the long-awaited messiah they had been waiting for, and even evangelicals bowed down and worshipped the beast.

Yes, there were Christians who simply viewed Trump as the lesser of two evils when compared to Hilary Clinton. Yes, there were Christians who were willing to give credit where credit was due while also calling Trump out on his behavior. Yes, there were Christians who couldn't bring themselves to vote for either candidate. However, there were plenty of Christians who loved Trump more than they loved God, and they sang his praises. Any criticism of Trump was met with hostility.

They hoped to fight fire with fire, darkness with darkness, evil with evil. However, they also hoped to fight spirit with flesh. They either forgot, never knew, or didn't care about what Paul said in Ephesians 6:12, "Our struggle is not against flesh and blood, but against the rulers, against the powers, against the world forces of this darkness, against the spiritual forces of wickedness in the heavenly places." To which, they were absolutely devasted when Trump lost the re-election in 2020. Their messiah was defeated, and hopes of a resurrection in 2024 are still clung to with religious fervor.

Even if Trump had been re-elected, what would happen if a Democrat won in 2024? 2028? 2032? Every election from there after? To whom would we place our hope in? How would we hope to preserve our American way of life? What hope would we have, period?

I, for one, am sick and tired of the notion "Either the country is going to repent or Jesus is coming back!" I spoke very heavily against the hybridization of Christianity and patriotism in *No Filter*, about those who can't separate the Apostles from the Founding Fathers or the Bible from the Bill of Rights, and it needs to be said again. Our rights as American citizens (or whatever other country you are a citizen of) do not negate our obligations as Heavenly citizens. Furthermore, the spiritual condition of the United States is not the measure by which we discern the second-coming of Christ. Are you so self-absorbed that you can't imagine God allowing you to live in a country in which you don't get your own way? Millions of Christians around the world have lived under such unpleasantness for centuries, and have even died as a result thereof. And yet, Christ has yet to return. What makes you feel so special?

When we are willing to forsake the command to love our neighbor as ourselves for the sake of telling our political opponents to "F**k off", we prove our hope isn't in the Kingdom of Heaven, but the kingdom of earth. When we preach the laws of man as though they were the doctrines of God, while dismissing the laws of God as the interpretations of men, we have already lost. The Apostles changed the more-depraved Roman empire by clinging to the truth of the Gospel, even to the point of death. If we hope to change the less-depraved United States, and the rest of the world, we are to do the same.

Even so, it will be a difficult task, especially if we lose our minds at the least bit of resistance and persecution. If the world is ever going to want what we have, what we have needs to be clearly and wonderfully displayed. If not, then how will they ever be convinced that what we have is better? If we ourselves don't live the way Christ calls us to live, then we need to take the log out of our own eye before addressing the splinter in our neighbor's eye.

I heard a testimony from a former Muslim expert who became a Christian. He said that after a particular debate with a Christian apologist over the reliability of the Qur'an, his trust in the Qur'an's reliability was completely shattered. Even so, he continued to argue for the Qur'an's reliability for another 10 years! Why? Because even though his faith in Islam was shattered, he wasn't yet convinced that Christianity was true.

Furthermore, he was terrified of what forsaking Islam would cost him (family, friends, livelihood, his very *life*, etc.) Thus, he wasn't willing to forsake Islam and embrace Christianity until not only his faith in Islam was shattered, not until he believed Christianity was true, but until he thought the cost of forsaking Islam was worth what he would gain through Christianity. That being, he wasn't willing to risk losing everything he had until he was convinced he would gain something better, just like the hypothetical man who finds the treasure in the field.

If we as the church act the same way as the world, react the same way as the world, and care about the same things as the world, then the world will stick with the devil they know rather than taking a chance to see whether the grass is greener on the other side. The Gospel doesn't conform to the culture, but confronts it, and we who proclaim the Gospel must do the same. If we want the world to change, we ourselves must be changed.

LAW VS LOVE

Unfortunately, most people don't want to change or improve themselves. They're like Cain, who instead of imitating his brother Able, chose to murder him. For it's easier to eliminate the competition than to emulate them. On the other hand, some people think the competition is unworthy of emulation to begin with, for there's nothing about their opponents to be found praiseworthy.

Inasmuch, one side or both wants to claim superiority in some form or fashion. The rich boast in their riches and the poor boast in their contentment. The strong boast in their strength, the wise in their wisdom, and the beautiful in their beauty. One side is superior to the other simply because they were born into that side. Achievement is boasted to be superior to inheritance, and inheritance is boasted in as if it were achievement.

However, there are those who boast when it comes to oppression and victimhood. Besides women and their feminism and the LGBTQ+ movement, there's also Intersectionality. Intersectionality claims that people are more deserving of status based on their victimhood. For example: A gay man has victimhood status when compared to a straight man. A black man has victimhood status when compared to a white man. A woman has victimhood status when compared to a man.

The more claims to victimhood you have, the more deserving you are of a job, a promotion, or simple pity. To which, a gay black woman certainly deserves a job more than a straight white man. Intersectionality divides everyone into one of two groups: oppressor and oppressed, with no exceptions. Apparently, worldviews are binary, but gender isn't.

However, who is more deserving of a job or promotion when it comes to the following: A *gay* white man, a straight *black* man, or a straight white *woman*? You could argue that black people have suffered worse than gays or women as far as intensity, but women have suffered at the hands of men from the creation of mankind. You could argue that women brought it upon themselves by eating the fruit first. But if Adam had done his job as a man, she wouldn't have eaten the fruit. Nevertheless, claiming that you deserve a job because of the past enslavement and mistreatment of your ancestors is a subjective claim. However, to claim that you have objective moral superiority because of past enslavement and mistreatment is null and void. You're not a morally better person than me in the present because of something my ancestor did in the past, nor are you justified in mistreating me.

Ezekiel 18: 14-23 says, "Now behold, he [an evil man] has a son who has observed all his father's sins which he committed, and observing *does not* do likewise. He does not eat at the mountain shrines or lift up his eyes to the idols of the house of Israel, or defile his neighbor's wife, or *oppress anyone*, or retain a pledge, or *commit robbery*, but he gives his bread to the hungry and covers the naked with clothing, he keeps his hand from the poor, does not take interest or increase, but executes My ordinances, and walks in My statutes; he will not die for his *father's* iniquity, he will surely live. As for his father, because he practiced extortion, robbed his brother and did what was not good among his people, behold, he will die for his iniquity.

Yet you say, 'Why should the son not bear the punishment for the father's iniquity?' When the son has practiced justice and righteousness and has observed all My statutes and done them, he shall surely live. The person who sins will die. <u>The son *will not* bear the punishment for the father's iniquity, nor will the father bear the punishment for the son's iniquity; the righteousness of the righteous will be upon himself, and the wickedness of the wicked will be upon himself</u>.

<u>But if *the wicked man turns* from all his sins which he has committed and observes all My statutes and practices justice and righteousness, he shall surely live; he shall not die</u>. All his transgressions which he has committed will not be remembered against him; because of his righteousness which he has practiced, he will live. <u>Do I have any *pleasure* in the death of the wicked</u>,' declares the Lord GOD, '<u>rather than that he should turn from his ways and live?</u>'"

Not even the oppressed are to punish the children of their oppressors for the oppression their fathers dealt against the oppressed. Furthermore, even the wicked who repent and practice righteousness will be forgiven by God, although they may still suffer the earthly consequences for their actions. Even Paul says in Romans 13 that the government doesn't bear the sword for nothing, and Christians shouldn't complain if they suffer for breaking the law, although there are some laws we should break, such as being forbidden to preach the Gospel.

Nevertheless, Jesus said we are to forgive those who have wronged us, whether they have repented of their wrongdoing or not, or else we ourselves will not be forgiven for our own sins. Also, we should pray that our enemies will repent and shouldn't desire their eternal destruction with glee, for God Himself doesn't desire from His heart that the wicked should perish but that they would repent. Do you desire to be less loving than God?

I'm not saying that everyone who buys into Intersectionality is wanting to bring harm to their opposition, but the peaceful ones typically don't do a good job at distancing themselves from the violent ones. You see, no matter what "noble" movement, organization, or institution you want to refer to, even among the church, there are only four types of people: Those who are true believers and think it's the best way to live and to love others as themselves, those who are in it for the sake of money, those who want to gain power (to destroy their enemies and/or control others), and those who simply want to belong somewhere and be accepted into a group.

The problem is this: No matter what movement, organization, or institution you want to question or be a part of, if you ask anyone within that group as to why they are a part of that group, they will almost always say, "because it's the best way to live and to love others as ourselves." No one, other than a contrarian or a cold-hearted idiot, would admit to not being a true believer of the noble cause, for in so doing, you make yourself out to be a target for those within and without the group.

If you want to make money, you've risked losing your job. If you wanted to gain power, you've risked losing it. If you wanted popularity, you've lost it, or at least gained it in the negative sense. Nevertheless, if you want to keep your money, position, or popularity, you have to learn how to mimic and argue like the true believers. Inasmuch, how can we tell who's a well-meaning sheep and who's a wolf in sheep's clothing? As Jesus said, you will know a tree by its fruit. (More on that in a moment)

The same dilemma is true with proponents of Critical Race Theory (CRT), which borrows ideas from Intersectionality, but focuses on race, mainly the struggle between black people and white people (and I say "black" because not everyone who identifies as black also identifies as African, and not all Africans are black).

However, just like any other "noble" cause, there are different beliefs among those who hold to CRT. Nevertheless, just like Intersectionality, there are only two groups: oppressor and oppressed. More specifically: racist and anti-racist. Furthermore, when figuring out who is oppressor and who is oppressed, the most common theme among CRT proponents is this: evidence is inferior to experience. That being, facts are inferior to feelings. Sound familiar? They claim that whenever the opposition (mainly white people) demand CRT followers to provide evidence, such is an exercise of white privilege. Furthermore, many CRT followers forbid their opposition (mainly white people) from even being allowed into the conversation. In their mind, the only white people who are allowed to speak are those who affirm the black experience as black people explain it, not those who provide evidence and statistics.

Their reasoning? Because white people speak from a position of power, and the American system is inherently racist towards people of color. Some go as far as to claim that math and science itself is racist. Some go as far as to say that working hard and being punctual is "whiteness" and shouldn't be modeled, even though the Bible commands us to work diligently. CRT doesn't focus so much on individuals, but systems. Given that the system in America was instituted by white people and black people on average are less successful than white people, the system itself is rigged and racist. To which, the only way to overcome racism in America is to overthrow the whole system and create a new one.

The most vocal of CRT followers reject the notion of gradual change and want an immediate overhaul. However, if history is of any value, cultures don't change overnight. In fact, even the Gospel with the power of God behind it took a few hundred years to change the Roman empire. The only time immediate change was successful was through military conquest, in which the opposition was destroyed. To which, if CRT, or even Intersectionality, wants to be successful, it would have to be through gradual cultural reforms or through military conquest. However, if you want to do so through military conquest, you are no better than the white people you hate so much (and they're not going to simply go down without a fight).

For hundreds of years, white Europeans boasted to being inherently superior to black Africans, which helped to justify their enslavement. However, there were African tribes who sided with the Europeans and helped to enslave rival tribes. Not only that, but the same happened with Native-Americans. Black Africans fought and enslaved themselves and Native-Americans fought and enslaved themselves long before white Europeans showed up. It's not that white people are completely evil and invincible bullies and minorities are completely innocent and helpless victims. For we're all bullies, and we're all evil, it's just that white people won the fight (although the chickens of white people's gloating and unsportsmanlike conduct are coming home to the roost of CRT and the like). Nevertheless, every bully has their own bully.

For white Europeans were once being oppressed and enslaved by the Ottoman empire, through which the story of Vlad the Impaler was given rise. His country, Walachia, an offshoot of Slovakia, was under Ottoman control, and it's from "Slavs" that we get the word "slaves". However, it was the Ottoman empire who brought an end to the Byzantine empire, which was what was left of the Eastern Roman empire. And the Roman empire was the empire which was in control of Israel during the time of Jesus and entertained themselves by watching slaves kill each other in the gladiatorial games. To which, was the Ottoman empire a villain or a hero? Either way, it doesn't matter to our current individual lives.

But what about the Romans? The whole passage of the Beatitudes in Matthew was about Jesus challenging, not catering to, the culture of Israel. Israel was a culture of Law in the time of Jesus. That being, they were concerned with keeping the minimum requirement of the Law of Moses, and such was the source of righteousness. For example: "The law says 'an eye for an eye.' I broke your window and I paid to have it fixed. We're even. Now, go away!"

The whole point of the sermon was to stop focusing on the outward and focus on the inward. Stop merely focusing on outward fornication and focus on your inward lust. Stop merely focusing on outward murder and focus on inward hatred. Stop merely focusing on obeying the Levitical Law and focus on loving your neighbor. However, everyone is included under the title of "neighbor", even your enemies. And in the case of the Romans, even your oppressors.

For Jesus said, "If your *neighbor* forces you to go one mile, go with him two." Jesus was referring to a Roman law in which a soldier could force a civilian to carry his armor for one mile. However, Jesus says that you should go two miles. What's the deal? Jesus was saying, "Stop viewing such laws as oppression and start viewing them as opportunity." That being, make the most of *any* opportunity for the sake of loving your neighbor as yourself, especially as an opportunity to share the Gospel. Yes, military conquest would have been a quicker method to establish Christianity, but it would have been at the expense of loving the Romans. Besides, Rome was eventually defeated militarily by the Huns, and it was Pope Leo I who convinced Attila the Hun to stop his conquest of the Romans in 452 AD. If Christianity itself isn't to be established through violence, then no other belief system is excused, whether it be colonialism, capitalism, communism, or CRT.

Nevertheless, if the American system is rigged against black people in favor of white people, why is it that first generation black immigrants from Africa are on average more successful than *white* people? From speaking to Africans, the common theme is this: They see America as a land of opportunity and make the most of it, whereas black Americans view America as a land of oppression and don't bother with it. Black Americans believe the system is rigged due to experience, but black Africans believe the system provides opportunity, as based on evidence. Perhaps that's why CRT followers don't like evidence (or successful black people who aren't CRT followers), because more often than not it proves them wrong.

Besides, even if the system was inherently racist, an abuser is not justified to abuse others because they were abused, first. A father can't beat his child simply because his own father beat *him*. Furthermore, what twisted father would tell his child he should be grateful for the beating simply because it wasn't as bad as the beatings his own father gave him? Inasmuch, if you can't beat your own child, how much less the child of another? Thus, even if CRT followers aren't talking about military conquest or the enslavement of white people, they're worldview isn't just incoherent with the Bible and the teachings of Jesus, but common sense.

How is it incoherent to the Bible? Because the Bible teaches that we are not to show favoritism. That is the whole point of the title of this book, *Balance*. We are to exercise fairness when dealing with people, regardless of their race or gender. We are not to refrain from hiring someone simply because they are a different race or gender than ourselves, nor are we to hire someone simply because they are a different race or gender than ourselves. Racism is evil, but so is tokenism.

[However, in the case of Jackie Robinson and baseball, maybe there does come a time for "tokenism". There were white people back then who said, "Let black people have their own league. Black people shouldn't be included in our league." Today, we think nothing of it to see black people, or any other race, in baseball and other sports. To this day, we still hear stories about someone being the first black this, or the first woman that. However, if Jackie Robinson was unathletic, he wouldn't have been the first black man in white baseball. That being, he wasn't hired simply for being black. Inasmuch, even if an organization wants to hire more black people, women, or whatever else, the people they hire should also be capable and qualified for the job.]

Nevertheless, CRT and Intersectionality focus far too heavily on whether or not something is racist or sexist, and those who oppose those ideas focus too heavily on whether or not their own actions fall under the category of racist or sexist. However, the point is not whether something is racist or sexist, but whether or not it's *loving*. If you shout at your neighbor saying, "I'm not a racist, you ***hole!" How are you loving your neighbor in saying such a thing? Besides, even if you could convince your neighbor that you're not a racist by definition, they'll still be convinced that you're the same insult that you just called them.

However, there are those who want to say the minority can't be racist against the majority, because the minority doesn't have power over the majority. That being, racism is only racism when there is power behind it. To which, the majority in power is worthy of contempt, whereas the minority has moral impunity. If such is the case, why do CRT and Intersectionality followers want power? Wouldn't *they* now be the evil ones, and it would be straight white people with victimhood status? Even if it's equality you desire, and not power, how will you determine the point at which you have reached equality? That being, at which point will it be possible to be racist towards white people or sexist towards men?

The problem with CRT, Intersectionality, and even Black Lives Matter, is that their creators are cultural Marxists. *Economic* Marxism/Communism separates everyone into two categories:

The bourgeoise (rich) and the proletariat (poor). Once again, no exceptions. It's completely binary. With *cultural* Marxism, they do away with rich and poor and replace it with oppressor and oppressed. (I reckon it's for the sake of allowing a rich black man to still claim victimhood status when compared to a poor white man. Sneaky sneaky.)

However, if there's a common theme with economic Marxism/ Communism, is that wherever it's implemented, things turn out bloody. And if there is a theme with economic Marxists/ Communists, is that whenever you point out the bloodshed, they dismiss it as "not real Marxism/Communism". To which, they promise that if their own Marxism/Communism is implemented, then things won't get bloody. Inasmuch, they agree that blood- shed is taking things too far. To which, I beg the question: How will you ensure that things won't turn out bloody other than altruistic promises that they won't turn out bloody? That being, what laws are you going to write and what institution will enforce those laws to ensure that things won't turn out bloody? (And if such is the case with economic Marxism, such should be the case with cultural Marxism.)

The problem is, no one ever answers that question, whether it be economic or cultural Marxism. Furthermore, those same groups want to defund the police, which would leave it to the citizens to defend themselves. However, they also want to take away our guns and villainize anyone who defends themselves from the mob. Not only that, but they don't condemn the angry mob, or they dismiss the violence and vandalism by saying, "It was *mostly* peaceful" or "not all black people" or "it's reparations for slavery". Yet, they justify such violence and vandalism because *all* white people are guilty of racism just by the color of their skin. If the leaders of such organizations don't think violence, theft, property damage, etc. is too excessive, and want you to be defenseless from such actions, why should we trust them to establish a fair and just system for all? If they're so destructive while not being in a position of "power", what should be the outcome if they receive the power they're demanding? As mentioned, you can judge a tree by its fruit.

Again, there are naïve and gullible people who believe such movements are noble at their core and we shouldn't dismiss the whole movement because of the excesses. To which, I agree, in that an organization shouldn't be completely dismissed or overhauled simply because some people within that group resort to violence to get their way. However, if such is the case, why not simply reform the current establishment and get rid of the excess? Why do you want to completely do away with the current system and come up with a completely new one? Typically, people want to change the rules to a game because they can't compete according to the rules. If you're wanting to create a completely new game, then don't get upset when I question your motives.

Nevertheless, it's easier to change a few rules in an existing game to make things fairer than to come up with a completely new game. And even if you insist on creating an entirely new game, no one likes to play a game in which the rules are not specifically written down for everyone to see and made concrete, or where the rules cannot be changed without an agreed upon amendment protocol. In so doing, the measure at which we can declare fairness and victory is clearly written down before the game is ever played. And any game in which only one team/individual is allowed to score and the opposition has to just sit there and accept defeat is not a fair game.

However, if you don't want to clearly define the rules before the game is played, why should I want to play? Besides, if the rules aren't clearly stated, then the rules are subjective. And if the rules of the game are subjective, then winning is subjective, and who is to say who has the upper hand? If evidence is not allowed and must give way to experience, then is my own experience (as a white man) credible? If we are going to start playing games of Majority vs Minority, or Oppressor vs Oppressed, how big is the playing field? Is it global? Continental? National? State? County? City? Neighborhood? Home? Individual?

Why is that important? Because, as a white man, I'm the majority in the United States, but not the globe. There are twice as many Chinese people than there are white people of all nationalities, combined. If I go to China, have an emergency, and I'm unable to get the help I need, am I a victim of racism? Is my white privilege still intact?

Or, I might be the majority in my city, but not my neighborhood. If my black neighbors were to break into my house and attack me, am I a victim of racism? Was my white privilege able to protect me? Do the terms racist, white privilege, majority, minority, power, or victim, mean anything at such a point? In times of emergency, I don't care about definitions. If I was to get hurt, I wouldn't care whether or not a Chinese doctor saw me as his equal, I would only care if he gave me equal medical treatment. I wouldn't really care what skin color my neighbors were or what their motives were, I simply don't want to be attacked.

Those who champion CRT claim that simply "not being racist" is still racist. You're not a non-racist until you are anti-racist. Meaning, you aren't innocent of racism unless you actively fight against racists and racism. To which, they actually make a fair point. As the parable of the good Samaritan points out, it isn't enough to simply not attack and rob someone, but to take care of those who have been attacked and robbed. However, in the case of the good Samaritan, the Samaritan was being hospitable towards his Jewish enemy, and we are to do likewise. If loving our neighbor as ourself means we are to be hospitable towards our enemies, how much less are we to attack them?

Nevertheless, if we take CRT thinking to its logical conclusion, then simply not being a "violent protester" is violence. You're not a peaceful protester unless you actively fight against violent protesters and violence. Even if you are a "true believer" and want to do things peacefully, then you must draw a clear line as to what defines "peace" and outright condemn anyone who crosses that line.

All in all, if you cannot (or will not) clearly define "how far is too far", or "at what point can the oppressor become the oppressed and the oppressed become the oppressor", then I don't care to take part in your silly, if not evil, game. If you refuse to condemn and remove the obvious wolves, how can I trust that you're not a wolf in sheep's clothing? If the church itself is to exercise discipline towards all members of the church, then no one from any organization is exempt of disciplinary action. A little yeast causes the whole lump of dough to rise. Until you remove the bad yeast, I will in all likelihood not care to listen to anything else you have to say.

Nevertheless, in practical terms, why should anyone care about the hearts and motives of those in charge of a system if the system itself historically treats everyone with fairness? However, to the credit of CRT and Intersectionality, the system in place isn't fair in all aspects. Black people on average receive harsher prison sentences when compared to white people, even for the same crimes. However, women on average receive lesser sentences than men. How is that fair and equal?

Now, some of those statistics can be owing to different laws for different states, the quality of lawyer the defendant was able to afford (which white people on average make more money than black people), etc. Nevertheless, there are a myriad of reasons for the differences, and they are worthy of discussion, not dismissal. Even so, the severity of the sentence doesn't excuse the committing of the crime. Each of us is to take personal responsibility for their actions, rather than shifting the blame onto others. [Read *The Blame Game* chapter in *No Filter* for more on the subject.]

Why do I bring this up? For my fellow Southern Baptist Convention is at war over the subjects of Intersectionality and CRT. Many within the convention have revealed themselves to be Woke, some as Anti-Woke, and some in between. Some are wanting to introduce Intersectionality and CRT as if they were the 28th and 29th books of the New Testament, and some don't want the two to even be discussed. There are those who think such ideas will be beneficial towards understanding the Bible, and there are others who think it will be detrimental. I shall argue against both notions.

Against Complete Inclusion: First off, if we are to conclude that anything can be beneficial in understanding the Bible, we would have to know what the Bible already says. For if we are to say that a statement in Intersectionality or CRT is a biblical concept, it's only because the Bible *already* makes such a statement. Inasmuch, why would we need Intersectionality or CRT to tell us what the Bible already says? Moreover, why on earth would we consider Intersectionality and CRT to be on equal standing with the Bible. The Bible is by default Biblical (obviously) whereas the other two take concepts from it and make it into something else, to which, the Constitution of the United States did the same thing.

However, as mentioned, we Christians shouldn't read the Bible through the lens of the Constitution, but we should be reading the Constitution through the lens of the Bible. Thus, neither should we read the Bible through the lens of Intersectionality or CRT, but the other way around. For the Bible is the lens through which we are to view everything. We wouldn't consider the Qur'an to be beneficial to understanding the Bible, would we? Of course, not!

Nor would you say the Qur'an should be taught in equal measure as the Bible.

Besides, if I were to say, "I disagree with Nazism as a whole, but there were some good elements in Nazism that we should consider when dealing with the Bible," I would be hated by all. However, the Nazi party was a socialist party, and almost all followers of Intersectionality and CRT are socialist or communist. To which, I'm certain that there would be parts of Nazism that they would think were good, even if they don't want to admit it in such terms. Inasmuch, there are those who react to the mentioning of Intersectionality and CRT in the same manner they react to the mentioning of Nazism.

Against Complete Exclusion: Although I abhor the overall notion and implementations of CRT and Intersectionality, that doesn't mean we should be silent about it. Even though it's a secular doctrine, are we to ignore it completely? Do we ignore the theory evolution or the Big Bang? Do we ignore the Mainstream Media? Hollywood? The global economy? The U.N.? The conflict between Israel and Palestine? China and Hong Kong? China and Taiwan? COVID 19? Political Elections? Of course, not.

Furthermore, even a blind squirrel finds a nut every now and then. I was once chastised because I said that I agreed with the statement "From everyone according to their ability, and to everyone according to their need". The chastiser pointed out that it was a quote from Karl Marx, author of *The Communist Manifesto*. If you couldn't already tell, I'm not a Communist. An obvious reason why I can't be a Communist is because Communism preaches against private property. If Jesus preached against private property, why would He command us to not steal? If there is no such thing as private property, then stealing is impossible. But regarding the quote in question, the statement is a Biblical statement. For Jesus commands that we are to do everything to the best of our ability, and He also commands us to help those in need.

Although I agree with many of the problems that Communism, CRT, and Intersectionality point out, I disagree with their solutions. However, the reality and recognition of those problems should give rise to fair and Biblical solutions, and we cannot come to those solutions if the problems are not allowed to be discussed. If the two subjects are not to be at all discussed, and all talks of dealing with racism and sexism are immediately accused as being Intersectionality or CRT, how will we ever move forward?

Besides, I enjoy listening to Dr. Jordan Peterson, and I have found his work to be very beneficial in my growth as a human being, and even as a Christian. For although I wouldn't dare claim him to be a Christian, given that he is "uncertain" about there being a God, much less whether or not Jesus physically rose from the dead, he does use the Bible and science when going into his lectures and debates. However, I don't view the Bible through his work, but I view his work through the Bible.

Nevertheless, his more abstract approach when teaching and critiquing the Bible has forced me to read the Bible even more so to make sure what the Bible actually teaches. It was the same when I stumbled across Christopher Hitchens. Even though he was a complete Atheist who rejected the Bible, claiming there was nothing good the Bible had to say that an Atheist couldn't also say, his criticism forced me to read the Bible to learn the answers to his questions.

Dr. Jordan Peterson has many followers, and Christopher Hitchens still has followers, even after his death. If so, it's because there's something about what they're saying that appeals to their followers. If we are to reach them, we have to be able to answer their questions. Not only that, but we have to show them that what Christ teaches is superior and is worth following. Inasmuch, we should do the same with Intersectionality and CRT. [End of debate]

Besides, there are plenty of black people who don't care for CRT or Intersectionality, but they still speak about reparations for slavery. And even if you can convince them that 40 acres and a mule was sufficient reparations for slavery, it doesn't make up for the oppression suffered under everything that followed, such as Jim Crow, the Civil rights movement, etc. There is also Black Liberation theology, which teaches that white people can't be saved unless they sell everything they have and give it to black people. There are those who support Black Lives Matter, a culturally Marxist organization that is also Pro-LGBTQ+, Pro-Choice, and anti-traditional nuclear family structure (I was able to take a screen shot of their mission statement before they took it down).

There are many political issues I could go further into, but I have spoken enough about issues of race, women, LGBTQ+, abortion, and other topics within this book and my other books to where the point should be clear. However, I want to bring back the topic of culture for a bit.

When dealing with the culture, there is a new phrase called "cultural appropriation". It's a phrase that means if someone from one culture capitalizes on an aspect of a different culture, you have appropriated that other culture, and such a thing is supposedly evil. Meaning, a white man can't sell tacos, because it further perpetuates "colonialism", where white people stole from other people groups to make money.

Hypothetical training exercise: Does that mean Latinos can't sell burgers? Even though I'm a white man, can I buy and eat a taco made by a Latino? If so, could I eat a taco that was freely given to me by a Latino? Can I buy products at a Latino store and make tacos for my own personal use? What If I bought more prod-ucts from the same Latino store to feed my family tacos? What if I bought even more products to feed a family reunion? What if one of my family members gave me $20 to cover the cost of the taco products? What if a stranger gave me $2 to make him a single taco? What if 100 strangers gave me $2 to make them a taco? What if a stranger gave me $200 to cater to his own family reunion? If not, think of all the money the Latino store wouldn't be making because I couldn't afford to buy their products and give tacos away for free. [End of exercise]

Furthermore, such people say a white man can't put on make-up to look like a black man, but can a black man make himself look like a white man? Some take it even further by saying a Mexican can't play a Hawaiian in a movie, or that an able-bodied person can't play someone in a wheelchair. They say a white man can't voice a black character in an animated movie. They say a straight person can't play a gay character in a movie. All in all, cultural appropria-tion is a politically correct way of bringing back segregation.

That being, white people should stick to white people stuff, black people should stick to black people stuff, etc. Everyone should be separated by color, culture, and class, all in the name of diversity and inclusion. We should be diverse on screen, but divorced in real life. Once again, those who are hostile towards God and truth become futile in their speculations.

Everyone has "appropriated" from other cultures at some point or another, and it was typically an expression of inclusion, not oppression. You can acquire things from other cultures by trade just as easily as acquiring them through colonization or empire building. Intermixing your culture with a different culture was often a sign that there was peace and harmony between the two cultures. I can borrow from you and you can borrow from me. I as a white man can make tacos, and you as a Latino can make burgers. In fact, let's make a burger taco or a taco burger! In fact, let's get married and have inter-racial children!

Mixing things up was often a way to express gratitude and appreciation for another culture. Yes, there were plenty of occasions throughout history when one group conquered another group to gain their resources, but trade was more common than empire building. The only reason we know about military conquests more so than trade agreements is because trade agreements are boring in history class and no one gets to accuse the other of evil-doing! The only trade agreements I recall learning in school was NAFTA and NATO, which were recent.

Be that as it may, being able to get along and enjoying each other's cultures and company is a far easier task than overthrowing the entire system and starting from scratch. A trade agreement is less bloody and more stable than a violent take over. However, when dealing with trade, we are to remember, a false balance is an abomination to the LORD, but a just weight is His delight. Our trade agreements should be fair, and our implementations should be equal. Although we can debate on what "equal opportunity" means, our goal should be to provide it to as many people as possible.

Inasmuch, unequal outcome is not by default evidence of unequal opportunity. A black child in America has more opportunity than a black child in Africa, and yet, black African children who come to America perform better than black American children. We can even the playing field to the highest degree, but the outcome is still a matter of personal responsibility and other factors that could be beyond our control.

Besides, even if we do take reparations into consideration, do reparations have to be in the form of cash? Can they not be in the form of programs? Would it not be better to teach someone how to fish rather than giving them a fish? However, many who demand reparations actually want quick cash. They're like a homeless person who claims to be down on their luck and needs a break. To which, when you offer to provide him whatever he needs, he refuses it and says, "I need money".

However, handing out a large sum of money to anyone, regardless of race, would more often be detrimental for their finances, not beneficial. How many stories do you hear of people winning the lottery and then not only spend it all on things of no eternal value, but end up in debt? A wise person can accomplish more with $1 than a fool with $1,000,000. (That is not to say everyone is a fool.)

If you were to give everyone in the country $50,000, there would be plenty who would use that money to pay off their debt, go to college or trade-school, invest in stocks, etc. I myself took advantage of living with my dad rent free while his disability checks paid for everything, to which I engulfed myself into watching sermons, podcasts, and writing my first book. Furthermore, after his death, his life insurance policy was the only way I was able to sustain myself during the COVID epidemic, and left me with a large safety net to stay at my lower-level job so I could focus on writing my second book and on recovering from some health issues. It also left me with a safety net to finally quit my job when new health issues arose, and allowed me to focus on recovery and writing *this* book. All these things helped me to become a better person and to gain focus in life. Thus, receiving $50,000 in cash can be a godsend for some people.

However, most people would waste $50,000 on buying a brand-new car they don't need, or a boat, a luxurious vacation, or something else. And afterwards, they would demand more money. To which, even though I'm willing to entertain talks of "reparations", I have no interest in reparations being in the form of money in their bank account. For I'm convinced it would do more harm than good. Not just for the people receiving reparations, but for the tax-payers as well. (Yes, there is plenty of wasteful and nonsensical spending going on in Capitol Hill, from Democrats *and* Republicans, but it doesn't mean we should add more wasteful spending on top of it. The national debt will eventually hurt all of us if not managed, no matter our race or ethnicity.)

However, even reparations in the form of programs won't accomplish anything on its own. For example: Black children on average have less access to quality education than white children. However, white people can pour money into black schools all they want, but unless they have equal quality teachers, it won't matter. Furthermore, if black children are convinced that the system is rigged against them, they won't feel motivated to apply them-selves in education, no matter how great the quality. To which, even if the notion of inherent systemic racism in America were indeed true, teaching it to your children will hurt them more than it helps them. The *current* system doesn't prevent black Africans from success, so neither should it prevent *you* from success. Like God said to Cain regarding Abel, "If you do well, will I not show you the same favor?"

What if white people started adopting black children? White people in America on average are more financially able to adopt children to begin with, and there are more white people in America than other races. If more adoption needs to take place to begin with, as mentioned in the last chapter, that would not only include white children, but black, Latino, Asian, and whoever else. Inasmuch, a massive generation of children from all races in this country would be given the exact same opportunity as white children. It would be more beneficial than probably any other program in this country.

However, I'm not so optimistic as to believe such a drastic measure would ever be taken, given the selfishness of human nature. I would like to reach a point to where I could personally adopt. However, God has laid Spanish-speaking ministry on my heart, and I have a strong feeling He will eventually call me to Central America. To which, I would probably adopt from there, not the United States.

Either way, I'm certain that if the day of adoption ever came, and the child was a child of color, there would be those among the Woke who would accuse me of cultural appropriation, and those among the Anti-Woke who would call me brainwashed by white guilt. Furthermore, such a mass adoption spree would be accused by some as white colonization all over again, for white people would be brainwashing a generation of minorities to think and behave as white people do, and such cannot be allowed! However, if thinking and behaving as white people do is dangerous, evil, or counter-productive to society, how then is it a privilege? Even if it's privilege because it gains me power, and the methods by which I gained power are evil, or if the acquisition of power over others is evil in itself, why then do you seek to gain power through the same methods? Even if you seek power through new or different methods, you are still seeking power.

We live in an imperfect world, and the problems of this world will have imperfect solutions. But that doesn't mean to not try our best at coming up with solutions. Jesus said the poor will always be with us, but that doesn't mean we don't try to help the poor. Jesus said there will be wars and rumors of wars, but He also said, "Blessed are the peacemakers." Jesus said we are to forgive those who wronged us, but He also said to seek to make restitution when we have wronged others. And lastly, no matter how we decide to right those wrongs, no matter who was wronged and who wronged them, everyone involved should have a voice. We need laws, but love is more important.

Just like an unfair game, if there is a trial in which one side demands that their voice should be the only voice allowed to speak, whereas the opposition is to remain silent, it's an unfair trial. If one side demands that only their evidence should be presented, whereas the opposition's evidence is to be dismissed, it's an unfair trial. If one side demands that only their witnesses are to be examined, whereas the opposition's witnesses are to be expelled, it's an unfair trial.

If someone is' making such claims, then such a person has no interest in fairness or justice. Why should we trust such people? We can't, we shouldn't, and we mustn't. If such is the case when it comes to justice, then such is the case with *social* justice. Whether it be whites or blacks, men or women, conservatives or liberals, Woke or Anti-Woke, Christian or non-Christian, any movement that demands to be the only voice to be heard while demanding the other side to be silent is not a fair and just movement. And such a movement and the laws they hope to put in place isn't driven by love. Inasmuch, it won't be long until the hatred begins to manifest itself, whether actively through violence, or passively through watching the violence unfold and doing nothing about it because it helps your own cause. And if you haven't figured it out by now, such is wickedness.

FLESH VS FAITH

Christians, as well as others, are afraid of "Cancel-Culture". They demand that they should be allowed to speak freely and to practice their beliefs with impunity. However, have Christians already forgotten that Christians were the first Cancel-Culture of America? That being, they wanted to silence anyone and everyone who wasn't living up to their ideal standards. Furthermore, there are Christians today who still want to do the same. Such people are called Theonomists.

Theonomy comes from the Greek words Theos (God) and nomos (Law). Theonomy is the belief that Divine law should be implemented in modern society, with some Theonomists wanting the Levitical law of Moses to be the law of the land (minus animal sacrifice and such). Inasmuch, many within the Christian church in the United States are convinced that our country should resemble what ancient Israel was to resemble. They believe the overall goal of the church is to lay hold of every facet of the culture, whether it be art, science, industry, or government.

Although I agree to the sentiment of Theonomy, I don't believe it's wise to force it down people's throats. As mentioned in the last chapter, the only way change can last is if it's done gradually through personal relationships, or done through military takeover. However, military takeover isn't an option for Christianity. If the first Jewish Christians weren't supposed to exercise violence against the pagan Roman government for the sake of Christ, then a Gentile Christian government is not to exercise violence against pagan American citizens for the sake of Christ.

Yes, Paul wrote in Romans 13 that the government doesn't bear the sword for nothing, but who does it bear the sword against? It is to bear the sword against foreign invaders and against those who harm the innocent. It doesn't bear the sword against practicing homosexuals, even though such a practice is an abomination before the Lord. It doesn't bear the sword against Hindus, even though they break the first and second commandment in worshipping other gods and idols.

I'm not saying that all Theonomists want to punish homosexuality and non-Christians as criminals, but there are some who do. The Puritans come to mind, and many Theonomists praise the Puritans, although they decry the Salem Witch Trials. To which, there are many Theonomists who are reasonable with their Theonomy, but they should do their best to distance themselves from the unreasonable in the same manner that non-violent protesters should distance themselves from the violent. If you're not willing to condemn the excesses of a movement, then why should we trust the movement as a whole?

Yet, if history is of any value, every time Christians established a theocracy, it soon turned into something more reminiscent of the fascism of Starship Troopers than it did the church. Unemployment, exile, imprisonment, torture, and execution, were the methods of dealing with not only undesirable behavior, but undesirable beliefs, as well. The church is to excommunicate unrepentant sinners from within the church (1 Corinthians 5 comes to mind), so would a Theocratic country have to exile criminals? What if other countries won't allow them into their country? What do we do with the sinners then?

Furthermore, what if the criminal repents? Do we welcome them back with open arms, regardless of their crimes? If Paul was to be welcomed into the church after repenting of killing Christians, then surely any other repentant criminal is to be fully welcomed back into society! Even if you're a Theonomist in whom your concept of theonomy is reasonable, who's to say *your* version of Theonomy is the one that will be established, much less continue to be exercised long after it's established?

Evil men used Communism as a humanitarian smoke screen to hide their ulterior motives and gain power, and there are "Christians" today and throughout history who do the same with Christianity. Even if the people who started the movement were well intentioned, it paved the way for the violent to quickly take over. Why? Because "Someone has got to ensure that the job gets done, and I'm the only one with the passion and resolve to get it done!" [Roaring applause].

Like Communism (and even Nazism), if you're a Christian who desires prosperity and protection above all else, you will align yourself with a charming personality who swears before Almighty God that they will provide prosperity and protection. And if you have an entire country willing to get behind such a person, may God have mercy on the souls who don't. Furthermore, who can blame such a soul for hating and resisting Christians who cheerfully desire such an outcome? All in all, like Communists today who dismiss the atrocities done in the name of Communism by saying "That wasn't real Communism," there are Christians today who dismiss the atrocities done in the name of Christ by saying, "That wasn't real Christianity/Theonomy".

However, there was a time when the people of God were to put homosexuals to death, but only if they were caught in the act of homosexual sex by two or more witnesses (Leviticus 20:13). They were not to condemn a homosexual to death because of his sexual attraction, but only if it was openly practiced. The people of God were to put to death those who worked on the Sabbath, such as someone carrying a bundle of sticks (Numbers 15: 32-36). However, Jesus points out that there are jobs that are necessary on the Sabbath (Matthew 12:5). Inasmuch, in both cases, the criminals knew the law and punishment before they committed the act, and yet, they still did it. That's what Leviticus 20:13 means when it says, "their blood will be on their own heads." (To which, the Theonomists still have an argument, albeit understandably terrifying for those who disagree).

On that note, there is something else to be addressed: There are those who say we should whisper where God has whispered and we should shout where God has shouted. They say that Jesus spoke more about greed than sexual sin, to which, we shouldn't be so vocal about the LGBTQ+ community and focus more on money issues. However, the Law of Moses didn't condemn the greedy to death, but homosexuals, adulterers, incestuous relationships, and those who commit bestiality. God destroyed Sodom and Gomorrah because of those sins.

Jude 5-7 says, "Now I want to remind you, though you know everything once and for all, that the Lord, after saving a people out of the land of Egypt, subsequently destroyed those who did not believe. And angels who did not keep their own domain but abandoned their proper dwelling place (Genesis 6:2), these He has kept in eternal restraints (Tartarus) under darkness for the judgment of the great day, just as <u>Sodom and Gomorrah and the cities around them, since they *in the same way* as these angels indulged in *sexual perversion and went after strange flesh*, are exhibited as an example in undergoing the punishment of eternal fire</u>."

Furthermore, Leviticus 18, which condemns incest, child sacrifice, homosexuality, and bestiality, starts with this paragraph: "Then the LORD spoke to Moses, saying, 'Speak to the sons of Israel and say to them, 'I am the LORD your God. <u>You shall not do what is done in the land of Egypt where you lived, nor are you to do what is done in the land of Canaan where I am bringing you</u>; you shall not walk in their statutes. You are to perform My judgments and keep My statutes, to live in accord with them; I am the LORD your God. So, you shall keep My statutes and My judgments, which, *if* a person follows them, then he will live by them; I am the LORD.'"

And Leviticus 18 ends with this paragraph: "<u>Do not defile your-selves by *any* of these things; for by *all these things* the nations which I am driving out from you have become defiled</u>. For the land has become defiled, therefore I have brought its punishment upon it, so the land has vomited out its inhabitants. But as for you, <u>you are to keep My statutes and My judgments, and you shall not do any of these *abominations*, neither the *native*, nor the *stranger* who resides among you</u> (for the people of the land who were there before you did all these *abominations*, and the land has become defiled), so that the land will not vomit you out should you defile it, as it has vomited out the nation which was there before you. <u>For whoever does *any* of these *abomina-tions*, those persons who do so shall be cut off from among their people. So, you are to keep your commitment to Me not to prac-tice any of the *abominable* customs which have been practiced before you, so that you do not defile yourselves with them</u>; I am the LORD your God."

I think the Bible does more than whisper about sexual sin. God destroyed entire cities and nations because of sexual sin. The reason why Jesus "whispered" about sexual sin during His time on earth was because the Israelites were well aware of the dangers of sexual sin. As to why Jesus said, "You have heard it said 'You shall not commit adultery' but I say anyone who looks at a woman lustfully has committed adultery in his heart". Also, Jesus went on to say what He said about divorce and remarriage being adultery. The Israelites agreed that adultery was wrong, but didn't understand what defined adultery.

The reason why Jesus "shouted" about greed was because the Israelites were obsessed with money. The Pharisees loved money more than God, and the people thought the Pharisees were the prime example of godliness. The Pharisees taught that wealth was a sign of favor with God, and the culture wanted to be rich. Jesus "shouted" about lust and greed because it was subtle and less obvious, not because it was worse than the obvious sins. Jesus spoke about the inner man more so than the outer man because matters of the inner man were completely ignored, whereas matters of the outer man were widely accepted by the Israelites.

But how could a loving God destroy entire cities because of their sin, or ever command His people to put certain sinners to death? The greater question is, why would a Holy, Holy, Holy God allow any sinner to live? Anyone who can't comprehend God's holiness doesn't comprehend sin's wickedness. Anyone who lacks having a fear of God also lacks having faith in God. As Proverbs points out, the fear of the Lord is the beginning of wisdom. But as Romans points out, those who oppose God become futile in their speculations.

But another question is: Why does God no longer command us to put sinners to death? Such is the question I hope to answer in this chapter. If we want to understand how we are supposed to live today, we need to understand why others lived the way they did in the past.

Adam: In Genesis, God created the human race from two individuals, Adam and Eve. Moreover, God made Adam from the dust of the earth, and from his rib He made Eve. Inasmuch, Adam couldn't boast in making Eve. As Paul put it in 1 Corinthians 11: 11-12, "However, in the Lord, neither is woman independent of

man, nor is man independent of woman. For as the woman orig-
inated from the man, so also the man has his birth through the
woman; and all things originate from God." They were to have
fellowship with God in the Garden of Eden, while also maintaining
the garden and subduing the rest of the earth to make it like the
garden. They were naked and unashamed. Moreover, Eve's name
means "Mother of all the living", for everyone who is born after
her will be her descendant. Also, Adam named all the animals.

However, Adam and Eve sin. God kills an animal and uses its skin
to clothe them. They are cast out of the garden and forced to
work the earth. They start having sons and daughters, with Cain
and Abel being the most prominent. Cain kills Abel out of jealousy
and is forced to live as a nomad. God promises Adam a righteous
son to take Abel's place, and Eve gives birth to Seth. The genealogies of Cain and Seth are the only ones mentioned out of the
other sons and daughters of Adam and Eve. Cain's genealogy is
marked by wickedness, especially with the account of Lamech,
whereas Seth had righteous Enoch and Noah.

Noah: However, by the time we get to Noah, all of mankind was
filled with violence and wickedness, to where God has Noah and
his sons build an Ark and preserve humanity and animals. After
the waters return to there previous state, God permits Noah and
mankind to eat any animal they want, but not with the blood.
God also institutes the death penalty for murder. He also creates
the rainbow as a sign to never flood the earth again. Noah then
blesses his three sons.

However, Noah's son Ham disgraces him by seeing his nakedness
(typically a Hebrew euphemism for sexual relations, but not for
certain in this instance). Noah is so upset he pronounces a curse
on Ham's son Canaan (whose descendants would make up the
land of Canaan). As the descendants of Noah multiply, they gather
at a single location, being of one language and one mind. They

decide to build a tower that will reach heaven for the sake of making a name for themselves.

God, knowing that nothing will be impossible for mankind if they are of the same language and mind, confuses their languages so they can't complete the tower and spread out across the earth. As mentioned in *No Filter*, if nothing would be impossible for sinful men to accomplish, then the spreading out of the people was a Godsend. (For the whole of humanity would have been at the mercy of a single dictatorship with weapons of mass destruction at their disposal. Furthermore, having to work together for the sake of protecting yourselves from a greater outside threat makes life somewhat tolerable within the ingroup).

Abraham: Out of all the people groups of the world (including Egypt) God chooses an individual man named Abram (who would later be named Abraham). Abraham's wife, Sarai (later Sarah) is old and barren, and yet, God promises Abraham that He will give the land of Canaan to his descendants, and his descendants will be as numerous as the stars in the sky and become a mighty nation. When Abraham asks why he can't receive it now, God tells him the iniquity of the Amorite isn't full yet. (God would soon destroy Sodom and Gomorrah. To which, God was basically saying, "Those in the land of Canaan are bad, but they're not Sodom and Gomorrah bad. At least, not yet.")

However, Sarah grows impatient and convinces Abraham to take her Egyptian slave, Hagar, and conceive a son through her. (Hagar was most likely given to her by Pharoah when he apologized for taking her in Genesis 12:16). Abraham then has a son through Hagar, named Ishmael. However, God tells him that he will have a child through Sarah. Even though Abraham begs God to make Ishmael the son of promise, God refuses. Afterwards, Sarah does indeed give birth to a son named Isaac, and afterwards God establishes the command for circumcision. However, Ishmael mocks

Isaac, to which Sarah wants Hagar and Ishmael sent away, and God agrees with Sarah, and Abraham does so.

But why? Because Ishmael was a son by natural means, whereas Isaac was by supernatural means. God didn't want to choose an already "self-established" nation like Egypt for His purposes, for He would make a nation from a single man and his wife. Not only that, but that nation wouldn't have even been possible unless God had opened Sarah's womb. Thus, the nation would be forced to give all the credit to God for their existence, not human effort, whereas Ishmael felt entitled as the first born.

Isaac: Isaac and his own wife, Rebekah, are unable to conceive for 20 years, and God finally opens her womb to conceive. However, it was a difficult pregnancy, to which God explains to her that she is carrying twins, and the twins would become their own nations. God explains that they are fighting each other within her womb, and the same would be true to life, not just among themselves, but among their descendants. God explains that the older will serve the younger, and she first gives birth to Esau (Edom) and then Jacob (Israel).

Romans 9 points out that God made the decision to choose Jacob over Esau while they were still in the womb, before either one had done anything good or bad. Why? Both grew up to be unsavory characters, so why Jacob over Esau? Why eventually Israel over Edom? Because Esau (Edom) would have felt entitled to the position, being the first born. Even the Israelites often felt entitled, and God would put them in their place (Deuteronomy 7).

Jacob: Jacob tricks Esau out of his birth right and has to flee from home in fear of retaliation. He goes to his uncle, Laban, and works for him for 20 years. In the meantime, he has 11 sons and a daughter with his four wives, and Benjamin was born after he fled his uncle's house. He would later wrestle with God for a whole night, and God would name him Israel, which means "Wrestles with God". For he contended with man and God and prevailed.

Joseph: Joseph has two dreams in which he rose to prominence over his brothers and they sell him into slavery out of jealousy. He ends up in Egypt and eventually becomes 2nd in command over Egypt and prepares for a foretold famine. His brothers come to Egypt during the famine and are reconciled with Joseph. The rest of the family moves to Egypt and stay there for four generations (Genesis 15:16) While in Egypt, the brothers become the 12 tribes of Israel. Reuben, Simeon, and Levi, lose their birthright because of previous actions, to which Judah, the fourth born, receives it after repenting for selling Joseph into slavery. ("And the scepter shall never depart from Judah." Genesis 49:10)

[Sidenote about 400 years of "slavery": Genesis 15: 13-16 says, "Then God said to Abram, 'Know for certain that your descendants will be strangers in a land that is not theirs, where they will be enslaved and oppressed for four hundred years. But I will also judge the nation whom they will serve, and afterward they will come out with many possessions. As for you, you shall go to your fathers in peace; you will be buried at a good old age. Then in the fourth generation they will return here, for the wrongdoing of the Amorite is not yet complete.'"

Seventy people went into Egypt during the famine, and one of them was Levi. Levi had a son named Kohath, who was also among the seventy. Kohath had a son named Amram, and Amram had Moses, making four generations until the exodus. However, Paul mentions in Galatians 3:17 that the law of Moses came 430 years after God promised that Abraham would have descendants. Meaning, there is no way they were enslaved for the total of the four hundred years. For God said they would be enslaved and *oppressed* for 400 years.

Furthermore, the same Pharoah who decides to enslave the Israelites and have their children put to death is the same Pharoah whose daughter would raise Moses. Moses was 80 years old when the exodus took place, ending the 400 years of oppression and fulfilling the promise of God to punish the nation the Israelites served. So, where does 400 years come from? If you start from when Isaac was persecuted by Ishmael, continuing into Jacob being on the run from Esau, who then had to run from his uncle, Laban, who then wrestles with God to become Israel, to Joseph being enslaved in Egypt, to the eventual enslavement of Israel and their liberation, it's a total of about 400 years. The promise to Abraham was 20 years before the birth of Isaac, meaning the Ten commandments were given 10 years after the Exodus. Thus, 430 years between the promise to Abraham and the Law of Moses.]

Moses: With the instruction of God, Moses then helps to establish Israel as a nation with laws for the sake of governance. Unlike Noah, they are forbidden to eat certain animals *as a nation*. Unlike Adam, who could wear whatever clothing he wanted, the Israelites were not to wear mixed fabrics. Unlike the other nations around them, they didn't have a king. However, if they were going to conduct themselves, they still needed judges, priests, and other officials. They also made the Ark of the Covenant and the Tabernacle.

The Levites, who would become the priests, wouldn't get any land as an inheritance, to which a tithe (a tenth, 10%) was needed and commanded from the rest of Israel to sustain them. Another tithe was required for the sake of the widows, orphans, poor, and foreigners visiting the land. And every three years, there was a 3rd tithe (which is super complicated to explain). To which, on average, a 23.3% tax was waged every year for the sake of paying the government officials' salaries and providing welfare for those who couldn't provide for themselves. (To which, if you're a

Theonomist who thinks we should have a government similar to Israel, you have to be at least *a little* Socialist).

Joshua: The Israelites enter the land of Canaan and start executing God's judgment on the Canaanites. Even so, God said beforehand in Exodus 23: 29-30, "I will not drive them out from you in a single year, so that the land will not become desolate and the animals of the field become too numerous for you. I will drive them out from you *little by little*, until you become fruitful and take possession of the land." To which, even during a time of military conquest, God knows it's better for His people to achieve victory little by little, or else they will be overwhelmed with managing everything.

But why military conquest? Why must they kill the opposition? Exodus 23 continues in verses 31-33, saying, "I will set your *boundary* from the Red Sea to the sea of the Philistines, and from the wilderness to the Euphrates River; for I will hand over the inhabitants of the land to you, and you will drive them out from you. You shall make no covenant with them or with their gods. They shall not live in your land, otherwise *they will make you sin against Me*; for if you serve their gods, *it is certain to be a snare to you.*"

God, who knows past, present, and future, knows that if the Israelites "coexist" with the other nations, they will forsake God and serve after their gods. They will forsake their customs and adopt the customs of the nations of which God judged them for. Deuteronomy 8: 19-20 says, "And it shall come about, if you ever forget the LORD your God and follow other gods and serve and worship them, I testify against you today that you will certainly perish. Like the nations that the LORD eliminates from you, so you shall perish, because you would not listen to the voice of the LORD your God."

God does not show partiality or favoritism. Even though the Israelites are God's chosen race and have special revelation, they are not excused for their sin. In fact, such revelation makes their sin more contemptable. God dealt patiently with the land of Canaan for over 400 years, but He wouldn't tolerate the sin of Israel for more than a few decades. Furthermore, such military conquest had boundaries, unlike Islam, which seeks to conquer the whole world. Israel was to be a nation set apart for God, a beacon of light by which the other nations would marvel.

For Deuteronomy 7: 12-17 says, "Then it shall come about, because you listen to these judgments and keep and do them, that the LORD your God will keep His covenant with you and His faithfulness which He swore to your forefathers. And He will love you, bless you, and make you numerous; He will also bless the fruit of your womb and the fruit of your ground, your grain, your new wine, and your oil, the newborn of your cattle and the offspring of your flock, in the land which He swore to your forefathers to give you. You shall be blessed above all peoples; there will be no sterile male or infertile female among you or among your cattle. And the LORD will remove from you all sickness; and He will not inflict upon you any of the harmful diseases of Egypt which you have known, but He will give them to all who hate you. You shall consume all the peoples whom the LORD your God will turn over to you; your eye shall not pity them, nor shall you serve their gods, for that would be a snare to you."

If Israel had been obedient to God, they would have had unexplainable prosperity, having an abundance of crops, no famines, no sickness, no infertility, no need for an army. For if anyone sought to harm them, the same plagues which came upon Egypt would come upon them. And the whole world would know "These are God's people". Furthermore, whenever a foreigner saw a man wearing pure fabrics who didn't shave his sideburns, they would know "This is an Israelite. Don't mess with him."

Judges: However, it would never be. Judges makes it clear that the people didn't obey God in destroying all the people they were to destroy. Their children would grow up and worship the gods of the other nations, and God would punish them for doing so. The time of the Judges was a time of perpetual sin, oppression, repentance, redemption, and turning back to sin. Even with the promises of God and the Law of Moses, Israel refused to be a nation set apart for God.

Saul: After a few centuries of futility, Israel reaches a point of desperation. However, they believe their problems will be solved in the appointing of a king. However, the main reason they want a king is to be like all the other nations around them. Essentially, they didn't want to be special anymore. Even though they have rejected God in their request, God appoints Saul from the tribe of *Benjamin* to be their king, whose life was marked by disobedience. God eventually rejects Saul as king and appoints David from the tribe of *Judah* to be king. And out of jealousy, Saul persecutes David the same way Cain did Abel, Ishmael to Isaac, Esau to Jacob, and Joseph's brothers to Joseph. For law hates and persecutes love. Flesh hates and persecutes faith. Saul is eventually killed in battle after reigning for 40 years.

David: Abner, the commander of Saul's army, fights against David for years for the sake of having prominence, using Saul's remaining son as a puppet to gain power. Abner is eventually defeated. Even though David was a man after God's own heart, he was still flawed. After committing adultery with Bathsheba and having her husband killed, God promises that his kingdom will be divided. However, even though David repents, the son born to him and Bathsheba dies.

(How that fits into "the son shall not die for the sins of the father" is worthy of discussion. In this instance, perhaps it was because the judgement came directly from God, not as a legal proceeding by man. Also, the event is possibly a foreshadowing of the Gospel. That being, in order for David's sin to be forgiven, the innocent son of David had to take his place. Or rather, when listening to the story of the stolen and slaughtered sheep, David says the man who stole the sheep deserves to die and should pay back what he stole four-fold, but David is the man in question, who stole Bathsheba and killed Uriah. To which, David loses four sons: the baby, Amnon, Absalom, and Adonijah. Maybe it falls under "the judgement you render unto others will be rendered unto you".)

Nevertheless, they later have another son named Solomon. David's son, Absalom, tries to take the throne from David and is killed. God promises to establish David's kingdom forever and chooses Solomon to be the next king, over all of David's older sons.

Solomon: After David dies, Adonijah, Solomon's brother, asks Solomon to give Abishag, David's concubine, to be his wife. Such a request was an attempt to gain the throne in those days, and knowing this, Solomon has Adonijah put to death. Even though Solomon's reign begins well by building the temple, replacing the tabernacle, he's eventually led astray to worship the gods of his foreign wives. God sends men to persecute Solomon for his actions for the rest of his life. God also decides that after Solomon's death He will split the kingdom of Israel into two parts. He chooses Jeroboam, one of Solomon's companions, to be king over the 11 northern tribes of Israel. He promises that if Jeroboam walks faithfully with God that He will establish his kingdom in the same manner he did for David. God allows Rehoboam, Solomon's son, to be king of Judah in the south. Solomon discovers that Jeroboam will take over the northern tribes and tries to have him killed, and Jeroboam flees to Egypt until Solomon's death.

Rehoboam: Rehoboam's pride and harshness towards his people is what ultimately led to the 11 tribes rebelling against him. They were tired and worn out from all the construction projects they had done for Solomon, but Rehoboam essentially told them in 1 Kings 12:14 "Shut up and do as you're told." The kingdom of Judah would go back and forth between having good kings and bad kings until the Babylonian Exile under Nebuchadnezzar and the destruction of Jerusalem and the temple.

Jeroboam: Even though Jeroboam returned from hiding in Egypt to be king over Israel, he didn't follow God. His kingdom would not be a lasting kingdom like David's. Furthermore, Israel would *never* have a righteous king over them. Eventually, Israel's wickedness became so great that God had it completely destroyed by the Assyrians and the people were scattered among the rest of the nations.

Gardens, arks, towers, families, cities, nations, promises, covenants, commandments, laws, altars, tabernacles, temples, miracles, conquests, prophets, judges, and kings, are of no benefit to those who hate God. If creation itself leaves the whole world without excuse, how much more so those who hear the voice of God but don't keep His commandments? That is why Jesus had to come and establish the church. Furthermore, that is why He had to establish the church the way He did and instruct it the way He did.

[Many in the prosperity gospel movements want to claim the church replaced Israel. Inasmuch, all the promises God made to Israel have been transferred to the church. They teach this to help justify their teachings of "If you have faith, God will reward you with earthly prosperity. If you don't have prosperity, it's because you don't have enough faith." But such is not the case, as explained later.]

God started the human race with two people. He restarted the human race after the flood with six people, and from them He created every nation. He chose a single individual to make a special nation from. He started Israel with twelve people. Jesus started his church with twelve people.

He made Adam from the dust and Eve from his rib. He had Sarah give birth to Isaac when she was 90 years old. He had a virgin give birth to the Messiah.

He confused the languages of the people when they were of one language and of one mind so they spread across the earth. When the disciples were of one mind, God sent the Holy Spirit to give them the ability to speak in tongues, so that all the different nations gathered at Pentecost would understand, and would spread out and make disciples among all the nations. When the Law was given, 3,000 people were killed, but when the Spirit was given, 3,000 people were saved.

Ishmael hated Isaac, Esau hated Jacob, Joseph's brothers hated Joseph, Saul hated David, Abner hated David, Absalom hated David, and Adonijah hated Solomon. Herod the Great, whose father was an Edomite and was appointed king of the Jews by the Romans, wanted to kill Jesus, even though he knew Jesus to be the King of kings and the long-awaited Messiah. The reign of Christ will endure forever, fulfilling the promise to establish the throne of David, forever. The Pharisees, who felt justified by the Law, wanted to kill Jesus, who confronted their religious hypocrisy. The people, for the most part, only followed Jesus because of His miracles and provision, not because they loved and kept His word.

The Israelites conquered their enemies with the sword, but the church was to convert their enemies with the sword of the Spirit, which is the word of God. The Israelites became a nation with laws and boundaries, but the church transcends nations, laws, and national boundaries. The world boasts in law and the flesh, but the church boasts in love and faith. The world hopes in safety and security, but the church hopes in God, even at the cost of safety and security. The church is better in every way than any-thing that came before it, and nothing better will come after-wards until the New Heavens and the New Earth.

For Jeremiah prophesied in 31: 31-34: "'Behold, days are coming,' declares the LORD, 'when I will make a *new covenant* with the house of Israel and the house of Judah, not like the covenant which I made with their fathers on the day I took them by the hand to bring them out of the land of Egypt, My covenant which they broke, although I was a husband to them,' declares the LORD. 'For this is the covenant which I will make with the house of Israel after those days,' declares the LORD: '<u>I will put My law within them and write it on their heart; and I will be their God, and they shall be My people. They will not teach again, each one his neighbor and each one his brother, saying, 'Know the LORD,' for they will all know Me, from the least of them to the greatest of them</u>,' declares the LORD, '<u>for I will forgive their wrongdoing, and their sin I will no longer remember</u>.'"

Why does the church want to recreate Israel in America? Why does it put its hope in making America great again? If anything, we should hope to make America godly as well as the rest of the world. However, such an outcome will not come through the enforcement of laws, but through the encouragement of love. It won't be through efforts of the flesh, but the exercising of faith.

God gave the Ten Commandments and the Law of Moses to the Israelites, alongside the performing of miracles and speaking to the people in a voice so terrifying the people were afraid they would die. And yet, they still wouldn't follow His ways. How then can the church expect to convince the country to follow God by shouting at them with a megaphone and waving protest signs? If the fear of God isn't enough to convince them to cooperate, the fear of government won't work either.

Yes, we should seek to influence government, media, art, science, industry, and all other platforms. Yes, it would be wonderful if a Christian Theocratic government could be *peacefully* established and maintained. Yes, it would be wonderful if the whole world followed suit.

But such is not the case. We share the world with others who do not think and believe as we do. Forcing the God-hating world to obey the creeds of the church will accomplish nothing. They will either want to resist and destroy it even more so than they already do, or they will simply pretend to behave. They will look and behave like Christians, but they won't be. They will look and appear as though they are alive, but they will be dead. Not only that, but the church will become complacent, feeling as though they've won. They may have won the country, but they will lose sight of what it means to be the church. Eventually, the façade will melt away, the love of many will grow cold, and the resentful subculture of darkness will rise once again. Oh wait, it already has.

Even though America was never a Theocracy, Christian ideals were mainstream for the most part. Hollywood and media gave the dark subculture a voice, and that voice has grown over the decades. Not only that, but it has become more and more appealing to each generation, to where we find ourselves where we are today. Why? It wasn't because the country lost sight of God, but because the church did.

We preached to love our neighbor as ourselves, but also wanted to conquer the Native-Americans for their resources. We preached that all men were made equal, meanwhile we treated black people as property. We preached against greed on Sunday, but we became more concerned about making money with the help of the industrial revolution. We preached against the wickedness of Hollywood to our children, but left the children alone to do nothing but watch TV all day while we worked to make sure we could afford a TV. If you can't govern your own household, you aren't allowed to govern the church. If you can't govern the church, you have no right to govern the country. He who is faithless with little will be faithless with much.

The country didn't forsake the church, but the church forsook their children. The country hasn't so much become too sensitive to the mistreatment of Native-Americans and blacks, but the church was too insensitive. Yes, the Woke takes things too far with their solutions, but it's a knee jerk reaction from centuries of callousness from the church. Yes, there were plenty of Christians in those days who wanted a peaceful solution, but the history of the world only remembers violence, not peace.

If the church wants to win the country, it first needs to win the church. If we can't even agree to sound doctrine and church discipline, how useful can we be? If church business meetings are chaotic, how much more so a government run by the church? Instead of screaming at each other about whether or not it's proper to kill babies, we will be screaming about whether or not it's proper to baptize them. Yes, abortion is far worse than baptism, but the same screaming and vitriol will continue over a more minor issue.

Nevertheless, if the church is concerned with safety and security, why will it ever take the risk of stirring the pot? If the church is more concerned about being liked by the culture than transforming it, it won't be transformed. Rather, it will continue to get worse.

TATTOOS VS THEOLOGY

Nevertheless, the culture is marked by certain trends that cause debate even amongst Christians as to whether we should participate in the trend. One of those trends is tattoos, and this trend sets up a training exercise that I want to explore in this final battle. Why should I dedicate a chapter about the seemingly insignificance of tattoos and the obvious significance of theology? Because such an exercise shall help to reveal the hearts of the readers in more ways than one. Humor me, will you?

First off, what does the Bible directly say about tattoos? There's only one verse in the Bible that talks about tattoos. Leviticus 19:28 says, "You shall not make any cuts in your body for the dead, nor make any tattoo marks on yourselves: I am the LORD." The word in Hebrew for *tattoo* is "qaaqa" and the phrase *mark on your-selves* is "kethobeth". Both words only occur once in the Bible. To which, given the single verse, there isn't much information to provide any context to the word. Some possible translations for *qaaqa* are an incision, imprint, or tattoo, and some translations for *kethobeth* are a letter, branded. Essentially, the verse prohibits an incision or imprint being branded onto your skin.

There are Egyptian mummies dating back to 3,000 BC with tattoos, and Moses was 1,500 BC. Thus, Moses and the Israelites would have been well aware of the concept of tattoos by the time Leviticus 19:28 was written. To which, it should be safe to say the command prohibits making any permanent cut or mark on your skin of any kind. Nevertheless, many claim that such a command was only for Israel, not the church.

However, it's interesting how so many people who are pro-tattoo have nothing to do with cutting themselves for the dead. I did meet a guy whose friend had died, and because he was too young to get a tattoo, he lightly carved his friend's initials into his shoulder with a safety pin. Unfortunately, doing so rendered him "psychologically unfit" to serve in the military, for it was "self-mutilation". As far as I could tell, he was a reasonable and rational human being. Even *if* such mutilation was a sin, it shouldn't have kept him from military service.

Having said that, there are those who are pro-tattoo who want to say that cutting yourself for the dead was a cult practice, as to why it was forbidden. If so, wouldn't tattoos have been a cult practice as well, given they're in the same sentence? And if cutting yourselves is a prohibition that continues to this day, why are tattoos perfectly fine? Either both were limited to the Israelites as a nation and permitted today under the new covenant, or they are both forbidden even unto today. So, you should either accept both, or abhor both.

However, the Hebrew word for dead is "nephesh" and it occurs multiple times in the Hebrew. Furthermore, it's definitions, depending on prefixes and suffixes, are various: a soul, living being, life, self, person, desire, passion, appetite, or emotion. Furthermore, soul and living being are not limited to humans, but extend to animals as well. However, given the specific suffix in this use of nephesh, it means a *dead* soul. Although, from what I can gather, there is no specification of whether it's only humans or *anything* that has died.

Aren't you glad for the suffix? Or else, you couldn't cut yourselves for the sake of recognizing humans, animals, life, desires, passions, appetites, or emotions. Such a prohibition would essentially forbid cutting yourself for anything and everything. Inasmuch, context is key. And in this context, the command is: "You shall not make any cuts in your body for the dead, nor <u>make any tattoo marks on yourselves</u>: I am the LORD."

Inasmuch, there is no prefix, suffix, or special condition regarding tattoos. Meaning, in all likelihood, tattoos were prohibited altogether, at least for Israel. However, there are other commands that shed light on the issue. Deuteronomy 20: 19-20 says that if you are at war, do not cut down any fruit trees, even for making siege weapons. But, if there was ever a time to cut down a fruit tree, wouldn't be for the sake of winning a battle?

Furthermore, Deuteronomy 23: 9-14 discusses how if you are at war, be sure to dig a hole before relieving yourself and bury the excrement afterwards. Yet, if there was ever a time to not waste time in burying excrement, wouldn't be when you are at war and need to be ready to move? Are there ever times in which there are exceptions?

Given that David was able to eat the priestly bread from the temple during an emergency, given that God requires mercy and not sacrifice, I'm certain that under *extreme* circumstances it's acceptable to cut down a perfectly good fruit tree or to not bury your excrement. However, I cannot imagine a situation where your life would literally be on the line if you didn't cut yourself or get a tattoo. Unless you were in prison and a gang forced you to get a tattoo or they would kill you, then getting a tattoo isn't a matter of life and death. Yet, even if it were a matter of life and death, it could still be a sin.

For example: The mark of the beast. Now, I don't believe the mark of the beast counts towards the argument of whether or not it's wrong to mark yourself or to get a tattoo of *any* kind. For the sin of receiving the mark of the beast is that you identify yourself as a worshiper of the beast, not that you marked yourself with cuts or ink. Furthermore, whether the mark is literally or metaphorically on your forehead or hand is up for debate. Also, whether or not the mark is a 666 or the actual name of the beast (in which the phonetic letters of his name become 666 numerically) is also for debate. However, if you're convinced the mark of the beast is an actual tattoo of 666 on your literal forehead or hand, then it's a sin to get such a tattoo, even if your life depended on it.

For Paul says in Romans 14: 14-23, "Therefore let's not judge one another anymore, but rather determine this: not to put an obstacle or a stumbling block in a brother's or sister's way. I know and am convinced in the Lord Jesus that nothing is unclean in itself; but to the one who thinks something is unclean [or sin], to that person it is unclean [or sin]. For if because of food [or tattoos] your brother or sister is hurt, you are no longer walking in accordance with love. Do not destroy with your choice of food [or tattoo] that person for whom Christ died. Therefore, do not let what is for you a good thing be spoken of as evil; for the kingdom of God is not eating and drinking [or getting tattoos], but righteousness and peace and joy in the Holy Spirit. For the one who serves Christ in this way is acceptable to God and approved by other people.

So then we pursue the things which make for peace and the building up of one another. Do not tear down the work of God for the sake of food [or tattoos]. *All things* indeed are clean, but they are evil for the person who eats [or tattoos themselves] and causes offense. It is good not to eat meat or to drink wine, or to do *anything* by which your brother or sister stumbles. The faith which you have, have as your own conviction before God. Happy is the one who does not condemn himself in what he approves. But the one who doubts is condemned if he eats [or gets a tattoo], because his eating [or decision] is not from faith; and *whatever* is not from faith is _sin_." (More on this subject and type of reasoning later.)

Getting back to the subject of context, what does the rest of Leviticus 19 say? I won't quote the whole chapter, for the numbering and placing of the chapters and verses of the Bible was done by men and men tend to be influenced by chapters and verses more so than they are influenced by the intention of the original author. (In case you were wondering, that's why I remove the numbers for the verses whenever I quote a text.) Remember, in the context of the Israelites, a new thought or subject was always prefixed with something comparative to the phrase "Now" or "Then", although not every use of those two words meant the beginning of a new thought or subject. Having said all that, let us continue.

Leviticus 19: 23-37 says, "_Now_ when you enter the land and plant all kinds of trees for food, then you shall count their fruit as forbidden. For three years it shall be forbidden to you; it shall not be eaten. And in the fourth year all its fruit shall be holy, an offering of praise to the LORD. But in the fifth year you shall eat its fruit, so that its yield may increase for you; I am the LORD your God.

You shall not eat any meat with the blood. You shall not practice divination nor soothsaying. You shall not round off the hairline of your heads, nor trim the edges of your beard. You shall not make any cuts in your body for the dead, nor make any tattoo marks on yourselves: I am the LORD.

Do not profane your daughter by making her a prostitute, so that the land does not fall into prostitution, and the land does not become full of outrageous sin. You shall keep My Sabbaths and revere My sanctuary; I am the LORD. Do not turn to mediums or spiritists; do not seek them out to be defiled by them. I am the LORD your God. You shall stand up in the presence of the grayheaded and honor elders, and you shall fear your God; I am the LORD.

When a stranger resides with you in your land, you shall not do him wrong. The stranger who resides with you shall be to you as the native among you, and you shall love him as yourself, for you were strangers in the land of Egypt; I am the LORD your God. <u>You shall do no wrong in judgment, in measurement of weight, or volume. You shall have accurate balances, accurate weights, an accurate ephah, and an accurate hin</u>; I am the LORD your God, who brought you out from the land of Egypt. So you shall keep all My statutes and all My ordinances, and do them; I am the LORD." (Fortunately, Leviticus 20 starts with "*Then* the Lord said to Moses".)

Now, there are plenty of different commands in this section, but I'm glad for it. For there are plenty of people who are against tattoos who aren't against rounding off their hairline or trimming the edges of our beards. They do not even bother to put in the effort to look up the Hebrew for the command to ensure they are reading it in proper context. They have no problem when it comes to hair, except maybe what Paul says about men having long hair and women having short hair.

Anti-Tattooists also don't care about whether or not you take fruit from a tree before the tree is at least three years old, nor do they care if the fruit that is taken from the tree the following year is consecrated to the Lord. Furthermore, although respecting your elders is admired, hardly anyone commands that you stand up in their presence. And lastly, hardly ever does anyone talk about not eating meat with the blood still in it, other than for health reasons.

However, we know that divination, soothsaying, mediums, and spiritists are forbidden in the church (Acts 19: 18-20, Galatians 5:

19-21) Remembering the Sabbath and keeping it holy is one of the 10 Commandments. Prostitution is forbidden, as well as deceiving and robbing people by having inaccurate measurements. And we know we should treat foreigners as we would ourselves or our fellow citizens. So, are tattoos among the commands that are no longer for today, or are they among the commands that were only for the Israelites? What if all these commands are for today and we've been sinning all this time? Who can say for certain?

The prohibition against blood is interesting. As mentioned, Noah was allowed to eat any animal he wanted, whereas the Israelites were prohibited from eating certain animals. However, both were prohibited from eating (or drinking) blood. Furthermore, even when the church was established and Christians could eat any animal they wanted, eating and drinking blood was still prohibited. For when the church gave instructions to the Gentile believers, they gave four instructions in Acts 15:19: to abstain from things sacrificed to idols, from blood, from things strangled, and from acts of sexual immorality.

Now, Paul talks a great deal in 1 Corinthians 8 about how the mature in Christ know that eating meat that has been sacrificed to idols is nothing, for idols are nothing. In so doing, he negates one of the four instructions that he himself helped to develop! Nevertheless, there are those who are immature and are convinced that an idol is actually something and they cannot eat meat sacrificed to an idol with a clear conscience. Paul says for the sake of the immature, do not lecture them for the sake of convincing them to eat. He also says he would rather never eat meat again for the sake of not causing a brother in Christ to stumble. Paul continues to talk about such matters in Chapters 9 and 10. These passages, along with Romans 14, should paint a clear picture as to how we should base our decisions regarding anything.

Thus, even if it were perfectly fine to get a tattoo for any reason, you shouldn't lecture a brother who is against tattoos to get one, nor should you get a tattoo to stir the pot. However, what you eat or drink can be easily hidden or temporarily put aside, but a tattoo is permanent. What if you want to go on a mission trip to a country that's hostile towards tattoos? (My own church visits such countries). Will you cover up your tattoo so as not to be a cause for division, or will you tell those legalists to get over themselves and flaunt your ink?

However, given that eating and drinking blood was prohibited for Noah and his descendants, and the New Testament reaffirms this without any later clarification from Paul or others, then it would be safe to assume that blood is still off the menu. Even if you want to debate about blood, no one except for the sexually immoral argues for sexual immorality. Not only is it prohibited by Paul, the other Biblical writers, and Jesus Himself, sexual immorality is prohibited in the passage talking about tattoos, albeit prostitution being specifically prohibited in that specific section.

So, in four New Testament prohibitions, at least one is wrong depending on context and one is wrong no matter what. To which, where do tattoos fit into the present day? The New Testament doesn't directly forbid tattoos, nor does it welcome them. Meaning, there is no clarification on tattoos outside of Leviticus 19:18. Meaning, whether or not a tattoo is acceptable today is a matter of your own conscience.

As for myself, given my own uncertainty, I could never get a tattoo. For if I was to get a tattoo while being uncertain about whether it's allowed today or not, I would do so with doubt. As Paul said, anything done in doubt isn't done in faith, and whatever isn't done in faith (conviction) is sin. Furthermore, even if I were convinced it were completely fine in itself, I do ministry work in countries that shun tattoos, and I have no desire to cause unnecessary friction and division. Having said that, I'm not your conscience, nor is anyone else.

In summary, when it comes to the Christian life, regarding anything, we have to consider four things:

1) The context of what is being discussed.

2) The matter of conscience and whether or not you're fully convinced that something is perfectly fine in itself.

3) Whether or not it's causing division, as discussed in Romans 14 and similar passages

4) 1 Corinthians 10:31: "Whether you eat or drink, or *whatever* you do, do *all* things for the glory of *God*."

So, whether you are pro-tattoo or anti-tattoo, consider these things: Are there certain contexts for tattoos or restrictions as to what kind of tattoos you can get? Even if getting a tattoo is perfectly fine today, are *you* convinced that it's fine? If you're convinced that tattoos are fine, are you going to pressure someone who isn't comfortable with tattoos to go against their conscience and get a tattoo? If someone isn't comfortable or disagrees with your tattoos, are you going to disregard their convictions, distance yourself from them, or become hostile towards them? If you're convinced that tattoos are wrong no matter what, are you going to disregard those who disagree with you, distance yourself from them, or become hostile towards them? And lastly, are you getting, or not getting, a tattoo for the glory of God?

Why do I bring up and devote an entire chapter to the discussion tattoos? Mainly for two reasons:

1) I see too many Christians getting tattoos without putting any thought into why they're getting them, other than "I'm free to do whatever I want!"

2) I have actually witnessed a street preacher chastising a passerby for having tattoos.

Both circumstances shed light on the greater issue. It is one thing to not scrutinize the matter of tattoos as greatly as I have in this chapter, but to have such an irreverent and indifferent attitude towards God and others such as "I'm free to do whatever I want" is typically present towards all matters in such a person's life. On the other hand, the same people who preach on the street corner and immediately rebuke a stranger for having tattoos are typically the same people who call women who dress a certain way a "whore", or call homeless people "pathetic", etc. before they have bothered to preach the cross and forgiveness.

I'm not against hellfire and brimstone preaching, but even Paul commended the deeply religious people of Athens in Acts 17 for their efforts in seeking God, even though they were breaking the first and second commandment by worshipping other gods and idols (which is a far greater concern than tattoos, dress, or work ethic). Furthermore, Jesus typically reserved such name calling for the religious leaders of His day whose legalistic nit-picking was creating a stumbling block for the people and preventing them from embracing salvation. Inasmuch, you strain out a gnat and swallow a camel.

Yes, calling out sin can make sinners angry, but if all you do is call out sin, all sinners do is get angry. Or, they despair and lose hope that they can ever be forgiven. Personally, I would rather have a tattoo that's a stumbling block for the preacher than preach in a manner that's a stumbling block for those who have tattoos, or practice anything that is without a doubt a sin. Jesus preached against sexual immorality, but prostitutes flocked to him. He preached against greed and extortion, but tax-collectors forsook their careers to follow him. Even though the rich young ruler walked away because of his greed, Jesus spoke to him from a place of compassion, not condemnation.

Whether you're indifferent or hostile towards pro-tattooists or anti-tattooists, the greater problem remains: If the church as a whole cannot find a peaceful resolution regarding tattoos, then there is nothing in which we will be able to find a peaceful solution. That being, if there is such hostility regarding tattoos, what hostility awaits regarding theology and anything in between? If we can't be civil towards our fellow Christians when discussing theological issues without seeking lawsuits through secular law, imagine how uncivil we'll become when such beliefs and attitudes are protected by Theocratic law? If we can't be civil amongst Christians, then God forbid if non-Christians are at our mercy.

If we can't even agree that the Bible is the default standard by which we judge everything else, what hope do we have? If we can't agree on which gifts of the Spirit are for today, or the manner in which they should be exercised, what hope do we have? If we place our hope in personal safety and security over the Gospel, what hope we have? What hope do non-Christians have?

If we value the culture or being counter-cultural over Christ, how can we hope to establish a culture that values Christ? If we cannot forgive and forget the past, how can we have a future? If we are more concerned about receiving what we feel entitled to rather than being concerned about loving our neighbor as ourselves, will not lawlessness ensue? If we are living according to the flesh rather than according to faith, then we are dead in our sins and should focus on getting ourselves right with God before we do anything else. Take the log out of your own eye, *then* you will see clearly as to how to remove the splinter from your neighbor's eye, Christian or non-Christian.

For Romans 2: 1-11 says, "Therefore you have no excuse, you foolish person, *everyone* of you who passes judgment; for in that matter in which you judge someone else, you condemn yourself; for you who judge practice the same things. And we know that the judgment of God rightly falls upon those who practice such things. But do you suppose this, you foolish person who passes judgment on those who practice such things, and yet does them as well, that you will escape the judgment of God? Or <u>do you think lightly of the riches of His kindness and restraint and patience, not knowing that the *kindness* of God leads you to repentance</u>?

But because of your stubbornness and unrepentant heart you are storing up wrath for yourself on the day of wrath and revelation of the righteous judgment of God, who WILL REPAY EACH PERSON ACCORDING TO HIS DEEDS: to those who by perseverance in doing good seek glory, honor, and immortality, He will give eternal life; but to those who are *self-serving* and *do not obey the truth*, but obey unrighteousness, He will give wrath and indignation. There will be tribulation and distress for every soul of mankind who does evil, for the Jew first and also for the Greek, but glory, honor, and peace to everyone who does what is good, to the Jew first and also to the Greek. For <u>there is no partiality with God</u>."

You should know by now that I'm not saying that we should never call out heresy. I'm not saying that we should never call out heretics by name, although I chose not to in this book. What I'm getting at is this: If you lack the ability to self-reflect, exercise humility, and surrender yourself to the Lordship of Christ as He has revealed Himself through the written word of Scripture, then God help anyone in whom you influence.

For even when it comes to theologians and their theological opponents, I am tired of people misrepresenting their opponents and making caricatures of their arguments. Even if the man truly is a heretic by what they actually teach, there is no need to make the person or the teaching appear to be worse than it already is. If I believe someone to be an angel, and you think them to be a devil, I naturally don't want to listen to what you have to say about them, nor am I inclined to believe you. Even if I'm convinced that there's a mole-hill, it won't help to scream at me that it's a mountain, even if it's indeed a mountain. Hardly ever does someone change their mind about someone they love in an instant unless they that person does something absolutely devastating. Even then, some people dig in their heels or hold out hope for redemption.

Typically, the only time a stubborn person ever recognizes that I'm right is when I make a prophecy over their life that comes true. Not that God actually gave me words to speak in an audible voice, but through the exercise of discernment, intuition, and the knowledge that you can only play with fire but for so long until you get burned. Inasmuch, I warn people that they're heading down a dangerous path, and they say I don't know what I'm talking about or that they know what they're doing and got it under control. However, pride and ego never lead to holiness and sanctification. Inasmuch, when my prophecy comes true, hardly ever do they start exercising humility or repentance. Sometimes, they outright avoid me, and sometimes everyone else, out of shame or denial. Nevertheless, I still do my best to avoid saying, "I told you so." There's no need to kick someone while they're down.

I once tried to convince someone that the person they were romantically interested in was a devil, but she thought he was an angel. I gave her countless stories of him being a devil, but she didn't believe it. Given the immediate situation going on during the conversation, I told her that he would do it again to a specific person within the next 5 minutes. As she was rebuking me for my "prophecy" he did it to the very person I said he would, right in front of her. However, even though she was now convinced he was a devil, she was also convinced it was her job to turn him into an angel. To which, I gave up.

I knew of a "man of God" who was a proven habitual liar regarding his testimony and so-called area of expertise. However, he was protected and defended by a powerful "evangelical darling" and continued to remain on his staff. When the evangelical darling died, I was certain his son would get rid of the man of God, now that he was in charge. Yet, *he* didn't get rid of him, either. To which, where there's smoke, there's fire. I knew that if Evangelical Darling Jr was continuing to protect and employ the man of God, then it meant one of two things: Either he didn't care about holiness and truth for the sake of friendship (Like Eli and his sons), or the man of God had dirt on him and was blackmailing him to secure his employment. Although I can't say for certain why the man of God kept his employment (and continues to keep it), it turns out that Evangelical Darling Jr is worse than the man of God.

There is no fellowship between Christ and Belial, remember? Thus, if someone is completely comfortable with a Belial in their midst, then Christ is nowhere to be found. Darkness hates the light. If the darkness doesn't resist you, then there is no light in you. Then again, even Satan masquerades as an angel of light. Inasmuch, such an imposter accuses the light of causing unnecessary division and conflict, asking that we simply all get along. All in all, I'm not saying we never call out the imposters, I'm just saying that not everyone you disagree with is an imposter.

Even the greatest of theologians aren't immune to chasing a heretical rabbit trail for a while. Name any theologian in history outside of the New Testament and I will show you a teaching that they taught or once taught that the current Wolf-spotters will say was inaccurate, or at least nonsensical. Thus, we shouldn't be so quick to assume that a previously reliable theologian, pastor, or celebrity who has recently left the theological reservation to have never been a brother to begin with. We rebuke them, we exhort them to return to the fold, and maybe even exercise church discipline if it gets serious. However, to immediately clump them into the group of imposters who have a history of being imposters will cause a lot of unnecessary heart ache for everyone involved.

Yes, if one part of the body hurts, the entire body hurts, but not every hurt is a deadly hurt. We shouldn't equate smacking your thumb with a hammer to a bullet to the head. Getting a tattoo shouldn't be treated with the same hostility as denying the resurrection. Naively supporting CRT is not the same as intentionally worshipping the Anti-Christ. Dipping your toe in the sea of heresy isn't the same as being a deadly man-eating shark.

However, that doesn't mean there isn't reason for concern when it comes to theological matters. For even though a harshly spoken truth can hurt, a kindly spoken heresy can kill you. A sword is more painful than a razor, but even a sword can pierce a non-vital part of the body, whereas a razor in the right location will kill you. A bullet to the head is less painful than stubbing your toe, but which would you prefer? Even if 99% of your body is healthy, if the other 1% is venom, then you will die unless you get rid of it.

Nevertheless, you can have all the right theology, but if you're self-righteous, then you will perish. Even if you hold to all the right doctrines, if you habitually and intentionally misrepresent your opponents for the sake of making them or their beliefs appear worse than they really are, you are not walking in the truth. If you live the entirety of your life habitually lying about your testimony, credentials, or anything else for the sake of being "impactful" for the kingdom of God, you will not enter it. All who practice falsehood shall perish.

JARS OF CLAY

So, what do we do with all this information? What do we do with all these troublemakers? Where do we go to get help? What do we do with ourselves? How could we ever hope to bring order to all the chaos? Fortunately, I prefer to leave my readers on a more positive and optimistic note.

Matthew 13: 31-32: "He presented another parable to them, saying, 'The kingdom of heaven is like a mustard seed, which a person took and sowed in his field; and this is smaller than all the other seeds, but when it is fully grown, it is larger than the garden plants and becomes a tree, so that THE BIRDS OF THE SKY come and NEST IN ITS BRANCHES.'"

So, to answer your questions, I shall leave you with the following: Jesus transformed the world with a ragtag bunch of blue-collar workers, a tax-collector, and a former terrorist. Jesus promised them and those who would come after them that He would be with us until the end of the age. If we abide in Him and He in us, as well as His word, whatever we ask of Him, He will do. However, if we are abiding in Christ, it will shape our prayer life.

We won't be praying for cars, houses, popularity, or such superficial things. We will be praying for supernatural things. Not that God will allow gold dust or glory clouds to fill the room, but that His word would move mightily in the hearts of men and women.

Yes, we should pray for spiritual gifts, but for the sake of edifying the church, not exalting ourselves.

For James 4: 1-10 says, "What causes quarrels and what causes fights among you? Is it not this, that your passions are at war within you? You desire and do not have, so you murder. You covet and cannot obtain, so you fight and quarrel. <u>You do not have, because you do not ask. You ask and do not receive, because you ask wrongly, to spend it on your passions.</u> You adulterous people! Do you not know that friendship with the world is enmity with God? Therefore, <u>whoever wishes to be a friend of the world makes himself an enemy of God</u>. Or do you suppose it is to no purpose that the Scripture says, 'He yearns jealously over the spirit that He has made to dwell in us'? But He gives more grace. Therefore, it says, 'God opposes the proud but gives grace to the humble.' Submit yourselves therefore to God. Resist the devil, and he will flee from you. <u>Draw near to God, and He will draw near to you.</u> Cleanse your hands, you sinners, and purify your hearts, you double-minded. Be wretched and mourn and weep. Let your laughter be turned to mourning and your joy to gloom. Humble yourselves before the Lord, and He will exalt you." (ESV)

If God refuses to give supernatural things to His children if they want to use them for their own purposes and pleasure, how much more so will He withhold natural things? Furthermore, if He can create the universe from nothing, mankind from dust, a nation from a barren womb, and a church from a virgin, why are you so convinced that you can't accomplish the purposes of God unless He blesses you with material abundance?

Jesus told the rich young ruler to sell everything he had and to follow Him. Meaning, if he obeyed, he would've had nothing. If the rich young ruler didn't need anything to follow Christ, then neither do you. Meaning, you don't need to become wealthy to be happy and content. Thus, you don't need someone else's wealth to be taken from them and be given to you. You don't need your debtors to pay off their debts to you. In fact, when we pray, we are to pray, "Forgive us our debts in the same manner in which we forgive our debtors." Inasmuch, Jesus teaches us that if you desire material gain, it is all you will receive. Meaning, if you should sue your neighbor to receive material restitution, that is all you shall receive.

I find the story in Luke 12: 13-34 fascinating: Now someone in the crowd said to Him, "Teacher, tell my brother to divide the family inheritance with me." But He said to him, "You there—who appointed Me a judge or arbitrator over the two of you?" But He said to them, "Beware, and be on your guard against every form of greed; for not even when one is affluent does his life consist of his possessions." And He told them a parable, saying, "The land of a rich man was very productive. And he began thinking to himself, saying, 'What shall I do, since I have no place to store my crops?' And he said, 'This is what I will do: I will tear down my barns and build larger ones, and I will store all my grain and my goods there. And I will say to myself, 'You have many goods stored up for many years to come; relax, eat, drink, and enjoy yourself!' But God said to him, 'You fool! This very night your soul is demanded of you; and as for all that you have prepared, who will own it now?' Such is the one who stores up treasure for himself, and is not rich in relation to God."

And He said to His disciples, "For this reason I tell you, do not worry about your life, as to what you are to eat; nor for your body, as to what you are to wear. For life is more than food, and the body is more than clothing. Consider the ravens, that they neither sow nor reap; they have no storeroom nor barn, and yet God feeds them; how much more valuable you are than the birds! And which of you by worrying can add a day to his life's span? Therefore, if you cannot do even a very little thing, why do you worry about the other things? Consider the lilies, how they grow:

they neither labor nor spin; but I tell you, not even Solomon in all his glory clothed himself like one of these. Now if God so clothes the grass in the field, which is alive today and tomorrow is thrown into the furnace, how much more will He clothe you? You of little faith! And do not seek what you are to eat and what you are to drink, and do not keep worrying. For all these things are what the nations of the world eagerly seek; and your Father knows that you need these things. But seek His kingdom, and these things will be provided to you. Do not be afraid, little flock, because your Father has chosen to give you the kingdom.

<u>Sell your possessions and give to charity; make yourselves money belts that do not wear out, an inexhaustible treasure in heaven, where no thief comes near nor does a moth destroy. For where your treasure is, there your heart will be also."</u>

Do you want to know if you struggle with greed? If not receiving money, from *any* source and for *any* reason, is breeding resentment, anger, bitterness, and hatred within you, then you are greedy. Just as the passage in James said, "What causes quarrels and what causes fights among you? Is it not this, that your passions are at war within you? You desire and do not have, so you murder. You covet and cannot obtain, so you fight and quarrel." If we don't need money at all, then we certainly don't need other people's money.

Nevertheless, even Paul worked for a living. Even Jesus said, "The worker is worthy of his wages." Most of us aren't called to be homeless, but not many of us need to be billionaires. That's probably why billionaires are so far and few between. Even then, we hardly need their own personal earnings, but the jobs and opportunities they provide. Yes, we could tax them more heavily and redistribute the money to those who have less, but how much more do they really need, and who makes sure they get it? California received $100 million to tackle the homeless problem, and it all went to people's salary. To which, even the "compassionate" are greedy.

But what I find so fascinating about the story in Luke is that a man approaches Jesus with a request that sounds like our typical prayer requests in Sunday school, and Jesus tells the man to deal with it himself. How much time and energy are spent praying and waiting for God to answer and God's attitude is, "What are you coming to Me, for? Get it, yourself!" That isn't to say that we don't pray for provision, for when we pray, we are to pray, "Give us our daily bread." However, mana isn't going to fall from the sky like it did Moses. You have to go out and get it. Pray for a job, but send applications. Pray for a spouse, but become the type of person someone would want to marry.

On the other hand, sometimes there are prayers in which we are powerless to do anything. No amount of praying will help you escape physical death. Even if you escape a particular type of death at a particular time, it's still appointed unto man once to die and then the judgement. To which, apart from the second coming of Christ, all of us will eventually die no matter what. So, what do you hope to accomplish until then? What do you hope God will say on that day?

However, there are times when we do pray and God answers, but not in the way we planned. I shall give my own parable (although inspired by someone else). "A man prayed for a cake, but he received milk. He came across another man who prayed the same, but he received eggs. They came across another man who prayed for a cake, but he received flour. They came across another man who prayed, but received sugar. To which, the four of them worked together to make a cake, and they split it among themselves. However, they came across another man who had prayed and received nothing, and in their pity, they gave him a slice."

That is how the church is supposed to function. That is why God gives different gifts to different people in different measures, so they will be forced to seek each other out and work together to reach the goal. So many people claim "I don't need church to fellowship with God". Maybe not, but you will not experience His fullness apart from the church. God provided for Elijah when he was alone by feeding him with the ravens and having him drink from the stream. However, He eventually dried up the stream so Elijah would have to leave and come across the widow and help her in her time of need. So, stop viewing the struggles of life as oppression and start viewing them as opportunity. If you pray for a tree, don't grumble when God gives you a seed.

Inasmuch, Jesus said in Matthew 17:20, "Truly I say to you, if you have faith the size of a mustard seed, you will say to this mountain, 'Move from here to there,' and it will move; and nothing will be impossible for you." If you are fully convinced that God has given you a promise, and/or gives you something small and insignificant in the eyes of men to accomplish the task, if you don't waver in your resolve, not even a mountain of an obstacle can stand in your way. However, in all likelihood, it will be little by little, day by day. But we mustn't lose heart. For even a seed that takes root can eventually split granite over time.

Besides, the human race, the nation of Israel, nor the church came about in a day. Furthermore, the church certainly won't be transformed in a day. However, *you* can be transformed. Your *family* can be transformed. Your *neighborhood* can be transformed. Your *city* or *town* can be transformed. Your *state* or *province* can be transformed. Your *country* can be transformed. Your *continent* can be transformed. The *whole world* can be transformed. However, it starts with you and the Gospel. Which, even now, you're probably still wondering "What's so special about me?"

This brings us back to the "earthen containers" statement. 2 Corinthians 4: 7-12 says, "But we have this treasure [the Gospel] in <u>earthen containers</u>, so that the extraordinary greatness of the power will be of God and not from ourselves; we are afflicted in every way, but not crushed; perplexed, but not despairing; persecuted, but not abandoned; struck down, but not destroyed; always carrying around in the body the dying of Jesus, so that the life of Jesus may also be revealed in our body. For we who live are constantly being handed over to death because of Jesus, so that the life of Jesus may also be revealed in our mortal flesh. So, death works in us, but life in you."

What does Paul mean when he writes that? "Earthen containers" is a fancy way of saying "jars of clay". What is so special about a jar of clay? First of all, a thief will think the same thing. If a lazy thief looks around after breaking into a house and sees nothing but pottery, he will simply move on, whereas only a diligent thief will bother to search the jars. Inasmuch, Satan is a thief, and he comes to steal, kill, and destroy. However, it isn't the jar of clay that's special, it's the treasure hidden inside it. The thief typically looks for treasure in a safe, a hidden box, a drawer, anything but a common jar of clay in plain sight. For who would be so foolish as to put a priceless treasure in a fragile clay jar?

However, 1 Corinthians 1: 18-31 says, "The word of the cross is folly to those who are perishing, but to us who are being saved it is the power of God. For it is written, 'I will destroy the wisdom of the wise, and the discernment of the discerning I will thwart.'

Where is the one who is wise? Where is the scribe? Where is the debater of this age? Has not God made foolish the wisdom of the world? For since, in the wisdom of God, the world did not know God through wisdom, it pleased God through the folly of what we preach to save those who believe. <u>For Jews demand signs and Greeks seek wisdom, but we preach Christ crucified, a stumbling</u>

block to Jews and folly to Gentiles, but to those who are called, both Jews and Greeks, Christ the power of God and the wisdom of God. For the foolishness of God is wiser than men, and the weakness of God is stronger than men.

For consider your calling, brothers: not many of you were wise according to worldly standards, not many were powerful, not many were of noble birth. But God chose what is foolish in the world to shame the wise; God chose what is weak in the world to shame the strong; God chose what is low and despised in the world, even things that are not, to bring to nothing things that are, so that no human being might boast in the presence of God. And because of Him you are in Christ Jesus, who became to us wisdom from God, righteousness and sanctification and redemption, so that, as it is written, 'Let the one who boasts, boast in the Lord.'"

The word of the cross is the Gospel, and the Gospel is the price-less treasure hidden in fragile jars of clay. Mankind was made from the clay, and yet, the God of heaven and earth chose mankind to overcome the works of the devil, mainly by becoming a man Himself. Isaiah 53 foretold that Jesus wouldn't be impressive in the eyes of men. While one earth, He was considered to be the illegitimate son of a poor carpenter in a town with a bad reputation. What could *He* ever accomplish?

He is the seed of the woman that would crush the head of the serpent. He was the seed from Abraham who would bless the nations. He is the Word made flesh, and He and His word are made known to us through the Gospel. The Gospel is the mustard seed which grows into something great. And if we have faith like a mustard seed, nothing can stop us. That precious seed is in a jar of clay. The seed of the Gospel is the greatest treasure we have to offer the world, and jars of clay are the perfect vessel to house such a treasure.

God's strength is perfected in our weakness. God's wisdom is perfected in the foolishness of the Gospel which we preach. We are not to be ashamed of the Gospel, for it is the power of God unto salvation for all who believe, to the Jew first, and also the Gentile. We are not to be ashamed of the Gospel, but emboldened by it.

John 3: 16-21: "For God so loved the world, that He gave His only Son, so that everyone who believes in Him will not perish, but have eternal life. For God did not send the Son into the world to judge the world, but so that the world might be saved through Him. The one who believes in Him is not judged; the one who does not believe has been judged *already*, because he has not believed in the name of the only Son of God. And this is the judgment, that the Light has come into the world, and people loved the darkness rather than the Light; for their deeds were evil. For everyone who does evil hates the Light, and does not come to the Light, so that his deeds will not be exposed. But the one who practices *the truth* comes to the Light, so that his deeds will be revealed as having been performed in God."

The light of Christ and the Gospel should be obvious in our lives. For Jesus said in Matthew 5: 14-16, "You are the light of the world. A city set on a hill cannot be hidden. Nor do people light a lamp and put it under a basket, but on a stand, and it gives light to all in the house. In the same way, let your light shine before others, so that they may see your good works and give glory to your Father who is in heaven." The world which loves the darkness will hate us because of the light of Christ within us, but fear not, it hated Christ first. Even so, we will not overcome the world of darkness in a day, but we can start by sharing that light in our own house. It's a great place to start.

Have Thine own way, Lord! Have Thine own way!

Thou art the Potter, I am the clay.

Mold me and make me after Thy will,

While I am waiting, yielded and still.

Have Thine own way, Lord! Have Thine own way!

Search me and try me, Master, today!

Whiter than snow, Lord, wash me just now,

As in Thy presence humbly I bow.

Have Thine own way, Lord! Have Thine own way!

Wounded and weary, help me, I pray!

Power, all power, surely is Thine!

Touch me and heal me, Savior divine.

Have Thine own way, Lord! Have Thine own way!

Hold o'er my being absolute sway!

Fill with Thy Spirit till all shall see

Christ only, always, living in me.

Adelaide A. Pollard 1907

CITATIONS

1) Metzger, Bruce M.; Coogan, Michael David, eds. (1993). *Oxford Companion to the Bible*. Oxford, England: Oxford University. p. 77. ISBN 978-0195046458.

2) Everybody Says Mark Was the First Gospel, But Was It? (With Dr. David Alan Black)–YouTube

3) Strong's Greek: 4202. πορνεία (porneia) — 25 Occurrences (biblehub.com)

4) Strong's Greek: 3431. μοιχεύω (moicheuó) — 15 Occurrences (biblehub.com)

5) Suicides Among American Indian/Alaska Natives — National Violent Death Reporting System, 18 States, 2003–2014 | MMWR (cdc.gov)

6) 23 Surprising Adoption Statistics & Facts for 2020 (2date4love.com)

7) https://www.All.org/learn/abortion/abortion-statistics/

8) Strong's Hebrew: 7085. עֲקָעַק (qaaqa) — 1 Occurrence (biblehub.com)

9) Strong's Hebrew: 3793. תָּבֹּתֶכ (kethobeth) — 1 Occurrence (biblehub.com)

10) https://www.bbc.com/news/science-environment-43230202

11) Strong's Hebrew: 5315. שֶׁפֶּנֹ (nephesh) — 754 Occurrences (biblehub.com)

[All scripture quotations are from the NASB unless othewise posted at the end of the quotation. Other translations include NIV and ESV.]